Ceramic Glazemaking

Experimental Formulation and Glaze Recipes

by Richard Behrens

A Ceramics Monthly Magazine Handbook
WILLIAM C. HUNT, Editor
MARK MECKLENBORG, Publisher
ROBERT L. CREAGER, Art Director

THE AMERICAN CERAMIC SOCIETY
Westerville, Ohio

Table of Contents

Foreword

This handbook is designed to provide the ceramic artist or craftsman with new glaze recipes and basic glazemaking information, as well as to suggest potential alterations for currently used glazes. Nearly all firing ranges are represented, which makes this volume a useful reference and source book regardless of the ceramist's present or future firing levels.

While much of the contents is adapted from information previously published in CERAM-ICS MONTHLY magazine, chapters have been compiled and updated with the latest research, and it is hoped this format will provide a more complete exploration of the topic.

Glaze proportions are given by weight, and each recipe totals 100 parts. This allows the glazemaker to measure ingredients in multiples or fractions of 100 grams, ounces, or pounds in order to easily vary the quantities desired. On an experimental basis, any proportion may be altered according to preference for various glaze qualities, and glazes may be tested outside of the stated cone range.

Several commercial frits are used in the following recipes, and the ceramist should be aware of these substitutions: Ferro 3134, Pemco 54, and Hommel 14 frits can be used interchangeably; Pemco 25, and Hommel 259 may also be substituted for one another.

While finished results may vary for a variety of reasons — mineral content in water, humidity, firing conditions, altitude, changes in ceramic materials, clay body composition, etc. — experimental testing should provide many successful glazes from recipes given here.

Richard Behrens

Part I
Glaze Formulation and Correction

A Simple Glazemaking Technique

BY COMBINING a series of different proportions of selected glaze materials and firing them to a known level, it is possible to determine mixtures suitable for use as glazes. While recipes may also be originated by chance, some knowledge about the function of a dozen or more materials can prove of considerable importance in the selection of compounds for testing.

Silica (flint), the essential foundation ingredient of a glaze, is present in amounts up to fifty per cent. Since silica melts at a temperature above 3000°F, it must be combined with elements such as sodium, potassium, lithium, boron, or calcium to lower its melting point to a practical firing level. Such glazes are satisfactory only if they remain vitreous and do not run off the vertical surfaces of ware. Alumina, usually contained in clays, feldspars, and frits, assures the proper flow of glaze. To obtain a broad spectrum of color, metallic oxides or carbonates may be added, as well as stains prepared from them.

Each element included in a glaze contributes certain characteristics — hardness, strength in tension, resistance to weathering or chemical attack, "fit" to a specific clay body, etc. The potter may, by his selection of materials, build in the properties desired.

For the potter who does not wish to involve himself deeply in the control or creation of glazes through the study of rules and chemical mathematics, there is an experimental technique which assures both functional and interesting glazes. He may use as a starting point various materials commonly available from ceramics supply houses; some of these fuse to functional glazes without additions of flux.

A number of materials — cryolite, sodium silicofluoride, wollastonite, Gerstley borate, cullet, wood ash, amblygonite, and dolomite — may be used as base ingredients for glaze composition. With additions of incremental amounts of kaolin, pyrophyllite, or flint they often produce good quality glazes.

Slip clays such as Albany and Barnard represent a combination of clay, feldspar, colorants, and other mineral ingredients deposited by glacial activity. They contain alumina and silica which are necessary for satisfactory fusion. In the stoneware levels of firing, fluxing (melting) agents suitable for experimental additions in smaller amounts include barium carbonate, whiting, strontium carbonate, lithium carbonate, magnesium carbonate, sodium silicofluoride, Gerstley borate, cryolite, wollastonite, spodumene, lepidolite, nepheline syenite, talc, ash, and most frits.

Functional glazes firing below the stoneware range may be formed by mixing known amounts of feldspars with fluxing materials containing large amounts of boron or lead. Commerically available frits may also be modified to establish a variety of functional glazes, and a number of frits may serve as low-temperature glazes without further additions. To produce glazes of good stability and aesthetic appeal, kaolin, pyrophyllite, flint, and other ingredients containing high percentages of alumina or silica may be combined with frit, using the incremental technique.

A simple method of establishing the necessary quantity of fluxing material is, for example: one hundred grams of feldspar are placed in a container and enough water added to provide a fluid slip. The first increment of fluxing material, e.g., five grams of whiting, is next thoroughly mixed into the feldspar slip, and a stripe of the resulting glaze applied with a small brush to a test pot or shard. Individual stripes are identified with an underglaze pencil or with a notation of dark slip or coloring oxide applied with a brush. For a more accurate assessment of glaze performance, another test stripe can be applied using two coats of the mixture. At this point, another 5-gram increment of flux is added to the feldspar slip and the above procedure repeated. A third, fourth, and fifth increment may also be tested. After tests have been fired to the desired temperature, an inspection should reveal which mixtures are potential glazes.

It is apparent that this experiment is not strictly accurate quantitatively. But, the range of firing of the average glaze, as well as possible small variations in the composition of materials, make the operation sufficiently accurate for its purposes.

Among other minerals of similar composition which may be tested in the same manner are: nepheline syenite, volcanic ash, Cornwall stone, spodumene, and lepidolite.

Although there are guidelines for optimum proportions of the elements used in a glaze, deviations from these norms may, nevertheless, produce useful and sometimes dramatic glazes. With the mastery of a few simple techniques, the artist-potter may compound a variety of unique and attractive complements for his ware. Recipes on the following pages may be incrementally altered to suit specific glaze requirements.

Four-Three-Two-One Glaze Formulation

THE FOUR-THREE-TWO-ONE METHOD is another simple and effective system for formulating glazes. This method calls for the combination by weight of four parts of any feldspar, three parts flint, two parts whiting, and one part kaolin (also called china clay). A variation of this method specifies four parts feldspar, three parts whiting, two parts flint, and one part kaolin. Such glazes are quite stable because they consist of alkaline metals, calcium, and ample amounts of alumina and silica. Glazes formulated by the four-three-two-one method have proved quite satisfactory when fired in the stoneware temperature range, and these recipes are simple to prepare.

Although this method was designed for use with feldspar, it is also valid if frit or select other minerals are substituted for feldspar.

A number of successful recipes based on the four-three-two-one method are offered here.

GLAZE I (Cone 6)
A stony matt glaze

Potash Feldspar	40
Flint	30
Whiting	20
Kaolin	10

GLAZE II (Cone 8)
A matt glaze

Potash Feldspar	40
Whiting	30
Flint	20
Kaolin	10

GLAZE III (Cone 1)
A translucent glaze

Gerstley Borate	40
Flint	30
Whiting	20
Kaolin	10

GLAZE IV (Cone 4)
A satin matt glaze

Gerstley Borate	40
Whiting	30
Flint	20
Kaolin	10

GLAZE V (Cone 1)
A translucent glaze

Spodumene	40
Flint	30
Whiting	20
Kaolin	10

GLAZE VI (Cone 4)
A satin matt glaze

Spodumene	40
Whiting	30
Flint	20
Kaolin	10

GLAZE VII (Cone 6)
A transparent glaze

Lepidolite	40
Flint	30
Whiting	20
Kaolin	10

GLAZE VIII (Cone 6)
A translucent glaze

Lepidolite 40
Whiting 30
Flint 20
Kaolin 10

GLAZE IX (Cone 8)
A matt glaze

Nepheline Syenite 40
Flint 30
Whiting 20
Kaolin 10

GLAZE X (Cone 8)
A stony matt glaze

Nepheline Syenite 40
Whiting 30
Flint 20
Kaolin 10

GLAZE XI (Cone 8)
A matt glaze

Volcanic Ash 40
Flint 30
Whiting 20
Kaolin 10

GLAZE XII (Cone 6)
A translucent glaze

Volcanic Ash 40
Whiting 30
Flint 20
Kaolin 10

GLAZE XIII (Cone 1)
A satin matt glaze

Frit 14 (Hommel) 40
Flint 30
Whiting 20
Kaolin 10

GLAZE XIV (Cone 1)
A satin matt glaze

Frit 14 (Hommel) 40
Whiting 30
Flint 20
Kaolin 10

GLAZE XV (Cone 1)
A satin matt glaze

Petalite 40
Flint 30
Whiting 20
Kaolin 10

GLAZE XVI (Cone 1)
A satin matt glaze

Petalite 40
Whiting 30
Flint 20
Kaolin 10

Changing the Fusion Levels of Glazes

BY REDUCING some principles of glaze chemistry to a few generalities, the potter may change a glaze composition to meet his needs.

Elements' Effect on Glazes

Alumina and Silica Both alumina and silica exercise control over the maturing point of a glaze. Alumina is more potent in this respect than is silica. Increasing the alumina or the silica in a glaze is a prime method of *increasing* the fusion point, but together they are even more effective. By the same token, the glaze maturing point can be *decreased* by lowering its content of alumina and silica.

Mixed Oxides A decrease in the maturing point of the glaze can be brought about by substituting a mixture of related oxides for a single one. Thus a glaze containing a substantial amount of calcium may have its cone-maturing-point dropped by substituting barium oxide, strontium oxide, magnesium oxide, or zinc oxide, in any combination. This would hold true for the alkali metals also. Substituting potassium oxide or lithium oxide, in different proportions, for sodium in a formula may accomplish a *reduced* fusion point. By removing one or more of such a mix, the maturing cone of a glaze may be *increased.*

Lead Lead oxide is a potent and extremely dependable fluxing material in glazes which mature below the Cone 6 level. Decreasing the lead content of a glaze and replacing this with an equivalent amount of the more refractory zinc, calcium, magnesium, or barium will tend to increase the glaze maturing temperature.

Alkali Metals The alkali metals, sodium, potassium, and lithium, are effective materials for dropping the fusion temperature of a glaze. Replacing the more refractory calcium, barium, magnesium, or zinc in the glaze, they act rather powerfully. Of the three metals, lithium is probably the most effective in that it does not increase the tendency of the glaze to craze as do sodium and potassium. While these metals are effective even in very low cone-maturing glazes, calcium, barium, and zinc are effective in the lower- and stoneware-temperature levels. Magnesium is effective in the stoneware level. By replacing some of the alkali metals in a glaze with calcium, barium, or magnesium, its fusion temperature can be increased.

Boric Oxide Boric oxide is a very strong fluxing material, acting throughout the range of firing temperatures. An increase in boron will decrease the fusion point of a glaze.

Materials Providing the Modifying Elements

Lead Aside from high-lead frits, the next most usual lead compound is white lead. Red or yellow lead oxides, or a lead silicate may also be employed. The novice potter should consider the toxicity of lead compounds and learn safe studio practices in conjunction with glaze calculation before attempting their use.

Alkali Metals Of the three alkali metals commonly used in glazes, lithium is superior because of its relative insolubility in water when its carbonate form is used. It also has the advantage of fluxing well and producing less crazing than does either sodium or potassium. Sodium and potassium are most often added to the glaze through the feldspars and these can be used to reduce the melting point of a glaze in the stoneware range of firing. For the lower cone glazes, they carry too much alumina and silica, and in that case, the melting point will increase. Soda ash (desiccated sodium carbonate, not bicarbonate) and niter (potassium nitrate) lend themselves to addition to glazes if their solubility is reduced by using an alcohol-water vehicle instead of straight water. This mix may be made by adding two ounces of water to three ounces of denatured alcohol or wood alcohol (methanol). Isopropanol may also be tried. If the rubbing variety is used, it should be used *without* mixing with water. This vehicle renders the solubility of the carbonate or nitrate so low that it is not a factor in glazing.

Alkaline Earth Metals Fluxes operating in the upper earthenware and the stoneware range of temperatures are found among the compounds of calcium, barium, strontium, zinc, and magnesium. These are mostly added as carbonates or oxides. Where such a mixture is present in the glaze, an equivalent replacement of one for the others may heighten the temperature at which the glaze matures. Used at lower temperatures with earthenware glazes, they may serve as a means of increasing the maturing point of the glaze to which they are added.

Boric Oxide Boric oxide is an effective flux which may be used at all temperatures commonly utilized in glazing. Colemanite and Gerstley borate are calcium-sodium-magnesium boron materials which are insoluble enough for introducing boron into the glaze. Borax, although soluble in water, is often introduced as a flux in a glaze. This can be rendered effectively insoluble if the vehicle used is the diluted alcohol-water mix already mentioned. Boric acid, having a relatively low solubility, can often be used effectively to introduce boric oxide into a glaze. It is very soluble in alcohol, so the diluted alcohol solution mentioned above should not be used.

Frits Frits are excellent means of introducing in the glaze insoluble lead, alkali metals, and boric oxide.

While economy may dictate the use of small test portions in making glaze tests, there are certain advantages in using a sample portion of no less than one hundred grams. Such a quantity is large enough to avoid small weighing errors.

When formulas used are in percentage units, these translate directly into grams and fractions thereof, thus avoiding paper calculations. After applying the glaze, you may wish to pour the residue into a plastic bucket. Over a period of time this collection of scrap glaze can be mixed, screened or ball-milled, and utilized to glaze ware.

Test surfaces may be provided by use of thrown or slab pots that are approximately four to six inches in diameter and with sides about three inches high. Free-standing test tiles may also be used. Some five to ten glaze portions may be brushed, poured, or dipped on a test. For dipping and good segregation of the test pieces, a bowl may be cut, while leather hard, into sectors like a pie. Each sector may be perforated with a small hole to enable the potter to wire or string a sample series together for subsequent study. The importance of using the same clay body in the preparation of the test pieces need hardly be pointed out to the potter who has had experience with glazes not fitting the actual ware.

Reducing or increasing the fusion level of a glaze involves the judgment of which material to select. Whenever possible, only one additive compound should be varied. As the experimenter's knowledge grows, more than one ingredient may be modified. Utilizing only percentage changes, the degree of change can well be of the order of about two to two and one-half per cent. Thus, if a boron glaze is to be reduced in its maturing point, some one hundred grams of the dry glaze may be prepared with additions of two and one-half, five, seven and one-half, ten, and twelve and one-half grams, etc., of Gerstley borate. These samples may then be fired in the kiln and, after cooling, the best composition selected. Occasionally it may be found that the percentage addition may not have been extended far enough so that another run with greater additions of fluxing or refractory material must be tried.

All records should be kept in a bound notebook. Great frustration can result from lost sheets of records from loose-leaf notebooks.

To point up the technique of carrying out test experiments in the modification of a glaze, a few examples may be cited. These represent fairly simple approaches which, in most cases, will produce the desired results.

Example 1 An attempt was made to secure a glaze maturing at Cone 1 from a Cone 4 glaze containing:

Colemanite 50.0
Kaolin 22.5
Flint 27.5

Six tests were made by adding two and one-half per cent colemanite, then five, seven and one-half, ten, twelve and one-half, and fifteen per cent. It was found that the ten per cent

addition proved most satisfactory.

Example 2 A Cone 8 glaze was dropped to Cone 6 by the addition of the medium-firing-range flux, zinc oxide. The composition of the original glaze was:

Potash Feldspar 48.2
Whiting 20.7
Kaolin 3.7
Flint 27.4

To one hundred grams of this dry glaze was added two per cent zinc oxide, then four, six, eight, ten, and twelve per cent. Fired at Cone 6, a ten per cent addition of zinc oxide seemed to produce a glaze which was similar to the original glaze.

The same glaze, maturing at Cone 8, was modified in an effort to change the fusion level to Cone 4. To this end, four, six, eight, ten, twelve, and fourteen per cent of boric acid was added to the 100-gram batches of the dry glaze. Satisfactory maturing of the glaze at Cone 4 was achieved with the sample containing the ten per cent addition.

Pinpoint control of glaze production can tax the skill of the qualified ceramic chemist. Approaching the problem of changing the maturing point of a glaze largely through craftsmanship, rather than through that of ceramic chemistry and physics, can be more laborious, but it does lie within the capabilities of the craftsman with the patience and will needed in controlled experimentation. Certainly it was through this procedure that the Chinese potters achieved their wonders.

Matting Glazes

WHEN A GLAZE is not shiny, when its ability to reflect light is reduced, it is called a matt glaze. The matt quality can be achieved when one of four conditions is present: undissolved particles suspended in the glaze, abrasion or chemical attack of the glaze surface, under-firing, and uniform suspensions of tiny "cryptocrystals" (buried crystals) in the glaze.

When a glaze saturated with a matting agent (whiting, for example) reaches its maturing temperature and starts to cool, tiny crystals begin to form, producing the comparatively smooth surfaces of satin matts. This crystal separation requires that cooling of the kiln be somewhat slowed; otherwise a clear, bright glaze may result.

Classification of Glazes

Glazes may be classified as acidic, neutral, and basic. The basic (more alkaline) glaze is characterized by the presence of considerable amounts of metallic compounds like barium, calcium, zinc, and magnesium. It is also likely that an alkaline glaze will have a reduced acidic content. (Acid constituents include silica, tin oxide, titanium dioxide, and zircon.) These materials are relatively insoluble which causes opacity in glazes when they "crystal out," or opaque and matt characteristics if the crystals remain suspended in the glaze.

Neutral glazes, being more chemically balanced between the basic and acidic, tend to be glassy and clear.

Tin oxide and zircon are used extensively in acidic glazes with tin oxide being considered the more pleasing. However, zircon is also widely used and serves very efficiently, although it must be added to the glaze in larger amounts than those needed to opacify and matt a glaze using tin.

Matting a Shiny Glaze

A practical method of preparing a matt glaze is to select a stable, shiny glaze and add a matting agent to it. The amount may be determined by adding, successively, equal increments of this agent to a known amount of that glaze, and then firing the tests to the temperature for which the shiny glaze was designed. Thus, a 100-gram batch may be measured into a container — a 2-cup kitchen measuring cup serves well. Water is added to the dry ingredients, and the glaze mixture is stirred to the usual consistency with a small, fairly stiff paintbrush. If the glaze is not viscous enough for brushing, a gum may be added. A small streak of this glaze is then brushed on the surface of a bisqued bowl, shard, or test tile, and the piece labeled with a ceramic marking pencil or with a narrow brush dipped in a dark glaze. About five grams of a matting agent are added to the remaining glaze, and this, in turn, is brushed on the test piece, labeled, and the process repeated with five more grams of matting agent added each time, until four or five samples are produced. The consistency of the glaze may be maintained by small additions of water, as needed. In theory, each addition or removal of material from the cup results in the introduction of an error, but in practice it is usually not enough to affect the results. A final, accurate composition may be determined when necessary, guided by the initial tests.

Matting Agents and Their
Effect on Glaze Color

Calcium carbonate (whiting) and *strontium carbonate* are similar in their matting action, and in their influence on glaze color. Both are excellent matting agents, although whiting is more widely used. Depending on the composition of the glaze, from twenty to forty per cent additions generally produce good satin matts, and in smaller amounts may result in transluscent matts. *Wollastonite,* a calcium silicate, often may be substituted for whiting as a matting agent, but it does have a flocculating (thickening) effect on glaze when used in sufficient concentrations.

When colored with four per cent red iron oxide, the calcium matts tend to be light yellow in predominantly alkaline glazes; in acidic glazes, a dark brown results. With three per cent copper carbonate, the alkaline calcium matts are turquoise, and in the acid state, a green is produced. Manganese carbonate in three per cent additions can give violet-brown matts, while in more acid conditions, a dark brown results. Cobalt carbonate added to an alkaline calcium matt tends to produce light blue, while a more violet-blue occurs in the more acidic glazes. Green chrome oxide, in one per cent additions to a basic calcium matt, will produce light green, while an acidic matt glaze may be a gray-green.

Barium carbonate has long been used as a cool, smooth matting agent. Barium-matted glazes tend toward an ochre color with four per cent red iron oxide added when alkaline, and toward yellow-brown under acidic conditions. With three per cent copper carbonate in an alkaline glaze, barium matting produces blue-greens which tend to be more green as the glaze is more acidic. Manganese carbonate, in an alkaline matt, tends to become dark brown under both acidic and basic conditions. With a one per cent cobalt carbonate addition, both acidic and alkaline glazes take on a blue hue. An alkaline barium matt produces a yellow to yellow-green as the glaze used is more acidic.

Zinc oxide matt glazes are among the most effective. Color changes are very common with zinc matting. When colored with four per cent red iron oxide, zinc matts tend toward orange-brown in alkaline glazes, while the acidic matts tend to take on a yellow-brown hue. Alkaline zinc matts are blue-green, while the acidic matts are light green when colored with three per cent copper carbonate. Manganese carbonate, in three per cent additions, produces violet-brown in alkaline zinc matts and dark brown in acidic matts. Cobalt carbonate in one per cent additions to a zinc matt, produces a luminous blue, while the blue darkens in a more acidic glaze.

Titanium dioxide holds a special place among the matting agents because of its ability to dissolve in the molten glaze and to recrystallize on cooling. Its effect on various constituents of the glaze is usually more powerful than the more common matting agents. Iron-oxide-colored alkaline glazes are yellowed by titanium dioxide, but light brown results when four per cent red iron oxide is added to an acidic glaze. Three per cent copper carbonate, in an alkaline titanium dioxide glaze, develops a turquoise hue, while in the more acidic types of glazes, a blue-green color is produced. Three per cent manganese carbonate added to a titanium-dioxide-matted glaze tends to be violet-brown in the more basic glazes, while a chocolate brown results when the glaze is more acidic. Cobalt carbonate, in one per cent amounts, will produce dark blues in an alkaline titanium-matted glaze, while a blue-green is found when a more acidic formula is used. One per cent green chrome oxide added to a basic titanium-dioxide-matted glaze yields green-brown tones, while a more grayish green results when the glaze is acidic.

Talc is an effective matting agent, producing smooth matt glazes. If four per cent red iron oxide is added to a talc-matted glaze, it yields pale yellow hues when alkaline and dark browns when acidic. Three per cent copper carbonate yields turquoise in an alkaline glaze, while a moss green results in an acidic glaze. Three per cent manganese carbonate tends to take on a milky hue in a talc-matted alkaline glaze, and is brown in the more acidic type. One per cent cobalt carbonate in an alkaline glaze takes on a light blue hue, while it is more violet in the acidic glaze. Green chrome oxide, added in one per cent amounts to a talc-matted glaze, produces light greens when alkaline, and green-browns when acidic.

Kaolin-matted glazes colored with four per cent red iron oxide, can produce red-browns in an alkaline glaze, and a more modulated hue in an acidic glaze. Three per cent copper carbonate in an alkaline glaze produces bottle green, while an acidic glaze yields a lighter green. A rust brown hue may be expected when three per cent manganese carbonate is used in an alkaline, kaolin-matted glaze. A darker brown results when this colorant is added to a more acidic glaze. When one per cent copper carbonate is added to an alkaline glaze, a luminous blue is produced. In an acidic glaze the color is more like pigeon blue. A moss green color is produced in an alkaline, kaolin-matted glaze with one per cent additions of green chrome oxide, while a lighter green is produced in the acidic glaze.

Common Glaze Faults and Their Correction

IN HIS CONTINUAL SEARCH for the means of artistic expression, the potter must resort to a certain amount of experimentation in his work with clay and glaze. Because of the nature of studio processes and materials, it stands to reason that the potter must expect faulting. The following are the common glaze faults and some corrective solutions:

Crazing Glazes which develop a network of fine or coarse cracks after firing are said to be crazed. Some crazing is intentionally induced as an embellishment to produce a crackle glaze and the cracks are sometimes carbonized, or filled with colorants (ink, dye, low-fire glaze) to emphasize their presence.

Crazing results from a lack of fit between glaze and clay body. When the glaze is in a heat-softened condition in the kiln, it may adhere to the clay without trouble; upon cooling, however, the glaze may contract *more* than the body and thus set up a strain between body and glaze. In short, while all solids expand when they are hot and contract when cool, the difference in shrinkage between clay body and covering glaze is sometimes too great. If this differential is substantial, the network of cracks might be finely meshed; if the strain is moderate or low, however, the network of cracks may be rather coarse.

Various techniques are used to correct crazing and these may involve changes in the composition of the glaze or the clay body, or, to a degree, modifications in the firing of ware. The artist-potter with average studio resources often must depend upon practical experimental procedures in determining corrections to eliminate crazing. A primary consideration in this determination is a change in the silica (flint) used in the glaze. In some cases the substitution of a finer mesh silica for a coarser variety may be enough to overcome crazing. Many ceramics suppliers stock a fine-mesh (small particle size) silica which is available at a slightly higher price than that charged for the regular flint. Or an *increase* in the amount of silica in the glaze may prove an effective way to eliminate crazing.

A practical and rapid method of determining the amount of silica which must be added in an effort to eliminate crazing may be carried out by a variation of the method described previously in "A Simple Glazemaking Technique." A 100-gram batch of glaze is weighed out and prepared for use, and two and one-half grams of extra silica (along with sufficient water to produce a good brushing consistency) is added to it, then mixed well and applied to a portion of a small pot. This is followed by the addition of another two and one-half grams of silica to the original batch, including a good mix and application to an adjoining area of the pot. This may be followed with one or two more applications, and in this manner a systematic increase in the silica content of the glaze can be quickly made and indicated with a marking pencil (or oxide wash) on the test piece. The pot may then be fired to the desired cone level and the results examined for evidence of crazing.

While an error is introduced each time an increment of silica is added to the glaze, an accurately weighed final test portion will pinpoint the exact amount needed. It should also be noted that an increase in firing temperature, from a half to a full cone, may eliminate any devitrification when extra silica is added to reduce crazing, or extra flux may be added to the glaze.

Crazing may also be reduced by increasing the silica content of the clay body to which the glaze is applied. By starting with a 100-gram batch of the clay body, small increments of flint may be wedged into it (much in the manner that silica was introduced into the glaze for testing). From this clay batch, small chunks may be removed and made into thin tiles and fired with some of the glaze to determine how much extra silica is needed to eliminate crazing.

An important aspect of obtaining freedom from crazing in a glaze is securing a good transitional interlayer between glaze and body. This occurs when the glaze chemically attacks the outer layer of the body and penetrates such pores as exist. The glaze interlayer so formed takes on some of the properties of the body, while that part of the body in close contact with the glaze becomes more glassy. In a sense, this layer may be looked upon as a type of buffer zone between glaze and body

which tends to reduce crazing.

The presence of calcium oxide in both body and glaze can facilitate the formation of a satisfactory interlayer. Additions of up to ten per cent whiting (calcium carbonate) to the body should be sufficient. Glazes containing significant amounts of such very active fluxes as lead, sodium, potassium, and particularly, boric oxide are effective in producing good bonding interlayers between glaze and body. The temperature and duration of firing also influence the effectiveness of an interlayer.

Where some variation in the character of the glaze is acceptable or sometimes desirable, the introduction of up to ten per cent whiting, magnesium carbonate, dolomite, zinc oxide, or kaolin may be tried. The optimum addition is governed by the degree of crazing, as well as the fluidity of the glaze. An experimental determination of the amount of additions of the various oxides may be carried out as described in the determination of silica percentages necessary to halt crazing.

Under some circumstances, firing to a higher temperature may result in a reduction of crazing tendencies. Heat shock or rapid cooling, particularly at the levels where silica changes from one state to another (called quartz inversion), may stimulate crazing. These stages of firing should be passed through slowly. It should also be mentioned that ware be allowed to cool in the kiln until it can be removed with the bare hands.

Shivering The reverse of crazing is shivering, the peeling of glaze from the body after firing. Measures used to combat this fault are the opposite of those utilized for crazing.

The first step that comes to mind in trying to remedy the shivering is a reduction of the silica content of the glaze. In some cases, a reduction in the silica content of the body may be of help. If some other approach seems more desirable, an increase in the alkaline oxide content can be counted on to reduce shivering tendencies. The most effective of these are sodium and potassium. Equivalent substitutions of nepheline syenite for feldspar, or ball clay for kaolin, are effective means for solving this glaze fault.

The experimental approach described under

crazing can be used effectively here for making incremental additions to the glazes or bodies being tested.

Crawling Crawling is a defect in which the fired glaze gathers into ridges, leaving some areas of the clay body uncovered. Crawling is sometimes described as beading, or curling. One cause of crawling is that excessive plasticity of the glaze tends to produce cracks as it dries on the ware. Such plasticity may be caused by excessive ball milling or the use of clays that are too plastic. A satisfactory test for correct fineness of materials might be considered to be a glaze that retains one per cent or less on a 125-mesh screen.

Another cause of crawling is improper storage of ware intended for glazing. A coating of dust may build up on the surface, or the ware may be handled excessively and acquire small deposits of skin oil, which can resist glaze adherence. The use of from one to three per cent suspending and adhesive agents such as bentonite or gums; and flocculating materials such as magnesium sulphate, calcium, or barium chloride, may aid in the application of the glaze and thus eliminate weakly covered spots which could result in crawling.

When pots are glazed inside (perhaps by the pouring method), then given a glaze application on the outside, some of the water from the exterior application may penetrate through the porous body enough to loosen some of the glaze that coats the inside surface; if this happens, portions may drop away, leaving blank spots which may cause crawling.

Drying shrinkage of glazes containing substantial amounts of zinc oxide, magnesium carbonate, white lead, and Gerstley borate may produce cracks which might open during firing to cause crawling. Calcining the zinc oxide may be helpful in such cases, or adding a little soda ash to the Gerstley borate glaze may reduce this tendency.

Among other causes of crawling the potter may wish to avoid are overfired pieces and "flashed" surfaces on bisqued wares which resist the proper application of glaze.

The application of a second coating of glaze over an initial coating which already is dry may bring about poor adherence and this, too, could lead to crawling. Cracks that occur in the glaze during the drying process may be filled by rubbing of the crack with a finger.

Soluble salts which migrate to the surface of the porous clay during drying, and can cause crawling, may be "fixed" in the body by the addition of a very small amount of barium carbonate to the dry clay batch.

Sponging pots with "hard" water may leave mineral deposits on the surface of the ware which may lead to subsequent crawling. An application of some neutralizing material such as vinegar may prevent this.

Pinholing Small "voids" which appear in the fired glaze may be due to the passage of vapor from the body of the ware or even from the glaze. A small bubble of air entrapped in the body during the conversion to its finished form may remain in the body to be liberated when it migrates through the molten glaze, leaving a small crater. This problem most often occurs with cast clay objects.

Pinholing may often occur when the viscosity of the glaze at the maturing temperature does not reach a fluidity sufficient to heal the craters. When the glaze contains combustible materials or a chemical composition which liberates gases as the glaze melts, pinholing may occur.

A number of remedial procedures involving both firing techniques and changes in glaze compositions can resolve most pinholing problems: (1) Reducing the speed of firing, or "soaking" the ware at the maturing temperature for half an hour or more may provide time for the molten glaze to flow into the pinholes and thus heal the defect. (2) Decreasing the thickness of the glaze may permit a more ready release of the gases which are causing the pinholes. Heavy applications of underglaze may liberate gases which leave pinholes when migrating through the covering glaze, also. (3) Reducing the amount of rutile and zinc, when present in any considerable amounts in a glaze, may be a help in eliminating this fault. (4) Substantial overfiring of a glaze may cause vaporization of some constituents which may cause pinholes to form in a glaze. (5) When the viscosity of the glaze is reduced by the inclusion of strong fluxing materials like borates, sodium oxide, or lead, the healing of pinholes is promoted. Controlled increments of the flux added to the glaze and then fired will indicate the amount of flux needed. (6) Finally, if reduction firing is started at lower temperatures, it may leave carbon deposits in the ware which may later turn to a gas at the higher temperatures and bring about pinholing.

Dunting This term is applied to a crack which tends to pass through both ware and glaze. As a fault, it is caused by thermal shock. Dunting usually occurs during the glaze firing, occasionally during the firing cycle, but more often during the cooling period. When dunting occurs during the heating cycle, it can be recognized because the edge of the crack will be somewhat smooth due to the melting of the glaze. If, on the other hand, the edges are sharp, dunting has occurred during the cooling process. The remedy for dunting is to fire slowly during the initial stages and to cool the kiln slowly. Ware should not be removed from the kiln until it can be handled with the bare hands.

There are two other suggestions that may be made about this glaze fault. Pots which have thick bases and much thinner cross sections in their upper sections may dunt if the ware is placed directly on the shelves for firing. This problem may be relieved by placing the pot on a stilt. When pots are thrown with curves of too-sharp a radius at the rim and at the foot, firing strains may induce dunting. Overfiring can also be instrumental in dunting. Dunting also occurs as a result of excessive silica content in the body.

Blistering There are times when a glaze is overfired and causes some of the glaze constituents to vaporize, with the formation of bubbles which burst and leave sharp, broken craters. This effect is known as blistering. One solution is to lower the firing temperature.

A "soaking" period at the end of the firing may also diminish or eliminate blistering.

Some Glaze Colorants

GLAZE COLORANTS, regardless of hue, are derived largely from compounds of a small number of metallic elements such as iron, cobalt, copper, nickel, manganese, or chromium. The compounds of these metals most commonly used are oxides and carbonates, but other colorants, classified as stains, represent prepared materials involving chemical combinations of these metals with a small variety of additional elements.

Glaze colorants can be applied directly on green or bisqued ware as underglaze, incorporated in a glaze, or applied over the glaze. The color produced is dependent on the colorant used, composition of the glaze associated with the colorant, the temperature of firing, and in some cases — the nature of the kiln atmosphere (oxidation or reduction) during firing.

COPPER

Copper is known to have been used as a glaze colorant in Egypt as early as 5000 years ago. In fairly neutral lead glazes it may produce a good green color, although its use in lead glazes is accompanied by an increase in potentially hazardous lead release. (Because of that tendency, the Lead Industries Association, Inc. does not recommend the use of copper as a stain or addition to any lead glaze intended for food contact surfaces.)

Various hues ranging from turquoise to clear blue are characteristic of the colors produced by copper glazes high in soda, potash, or lithium. Copper glazes containing high barium levels can produce pronounced ultramarine colors. In the stoneware firing temperatures, copper colorants have a tendency to volatilize rather strongly.

Three copper compounds are commonly used as colorants. These are black copper oxide (CuO), red copper oxide (Cu_2O), and copper carbonate ($CuCO_3$). Of the three, copper carbonate lends itself well to glaze use. Red copper oxide, while having a high tinting power, is seldom used as a colorant. Black copper oxide is extensively used but sometimes lacks the dispersing power of the carbonate. Copper colorants, in additions of one per cent, will produce light tints, while two or three per cent additions will produce medium to strong glaze color. Five per cent or more can produce dark, metallic surfaces.

Copper reds, produced by properly managed reduction firing of copper glazes, result in red coloration sometimes known as peach bloom, oxblood, and flambe. The brightest reds of copper reduction result when the glaze is fairly fluid at the maturing point — often a characteristic of the more alkaline glazes. Matting agents like magnesium, barium, or alumina, when present in sufficient amount, may lead to muddying of the glaze. Small amounts of copper colorant, up to one per cent, produce the most brilliant reds.

A number of copper-influenced glaze recipes may be of interest:

GLAZE I (Cone 014)
A glassy, greenish blue glaze

Sodium Silicofluoride	35.6
Frit 14 (Hommel)	36.0
Kaolin	19.3
Flint	9.1
Add: Copper Carbonate	3.0

GLAZE II (Cone 06)
A bright, turquoise glaze

Colemanite	47.0
Whiting	3.0
Volcanic Ash	50.0
Add: Copper Carbonate	3.0

GLAZE III (Cone 4)
An ultramarine, matt glaze

Barium Carbonate	52.5
Spodumene	47.5
Add: Copper Carbonate	3.0
Bentonite	2.0

GLAZE IV (Cone 4)
A patterned, greenish black glaze

Whiting	26.7
Lepidolite	31.8
Spodumene	17.2
Flint	24.3
Add: Copper Carbonate	3.0
Bentonite	2.0

GLAZE V (Cone 6 reduction)
A bright, copper red glaze

Lithium Carbonate	15.2
Whiting	8.2
Potash Feldspar	57.0
Kaolin	2.5
Flint	17.1
Add: Copper Carbonate	0.5
Tin Oxide	2.0

GLAZE VI (Cone 9 reduction)
A bright, copper red glaze

Colemanite	19.3
Spodumene	36.0
Kaolin	9.9
Flint	34.8
Add: Copper Carbonate	0.5
Tin Oxide	2.0

IRON

Iron is predominant among the various colorant metals. In its various mineral forms, iron constitutes at least five per cent of the outer mantle of the earth. Its acceptance as a prime colorant may, in part, be due to its ability to produce soft earthy colors and thus relate aesthetically to the clay medium.

Among the early glaze colorants were the natural mineral iron earths. These are well known to the artist by such names as ochre, sienna, and umber. Crocus Martis, similar to these in its content of iron, has also been frequently used as a colorant. These represent natural iron ores containing various amounts of hydrated iron oxide, clay, sand, calcium carbonate (whiting), and sometimes manganese and small amounts of other oxides. These natural minerals vary somewhat from the color obtained when chemically refined iron oxide is used.

Red and black iron oxide most commonly function as prime colorants. Red iron oxide (Fe_2O_3) is fine in particle size and disperses well when added to glaze or slip. Black iron oxide (Fe_3O_4), the magnetic oxide of iron, is much like the red oxide in use. The black oxide is often not pulverized as finely as the red oxide. This may not be an advantage if a well-dispersed color is desired. The elemental iron content of black iron oxide is somewhat higher than that of the red so its tinting power is somewhat greater. A warm iron red pigment, extensively used for overglaze decoration at a very low firing temperature, may be prepared by calcining iron sulphate ($FeSO_4 \cdot 7H_2O$) at a low temperature. The temperature of firing this green sulphate determines the warmth of iron color produced. The crystals of this inexpensive salt are first crushed and sieved to about 16- or 20-mesh, spread in a shallow dish, and fired to Cone 021 (oxidation). A small amount of sulphurous fumes is released and a nasturtium red color results. When calcined at Cone 020 a coral tint develops, a Cone 018 firing produces a raspberry red, at Cone 015 an orchid red tint is produced, and at Cone 06 a violet tone results. These colorants can be used with low temperature lead borosilicate glazes or a nonleaded glaze based on a boron flux. If the latter is preferred, the solubility of the boric oxide may be reduced to an acceptable level by using ice water as the vehicle. Lead frits such as Hommel 33 may also be utilized where the ware is not to be used to hold food.

Iron oxide may, in oxidation, produce light straw or tan coloration, depending somewhat on the composition of the glaze with one to two per cent additions of the oxide. Additions from three to five per cent will produce tan or brown, while seven to ten per cent additions may produce color ranging from brown to brownish black.

Glazes containing two per cent or less iron, when fired in reduction, will produce a cool green celadon or an olive hue. Larger additions of iron in the seven to ten per cent range, may produce khaki and red to deep brown tones when reduced. Often when the glaze contains the higher percentages of iron, crystalline patterns appear in the glaze; or if reoxidized during cooling, the process may yield bright iron reds.

A number of iron colored glazes may prove of interest:

GLAZE VII (Cone 015)
A bright, brown glaze

Colemanite	27.5
Lithium Carbonate	7.8
Frit 25 (Pemco)	38.3
Kaolin	15.5
Flint	10.9
Add: Red Iron Oxide	5.0
Bentonite	2.0

GLAZE VIII (Cone 1)
An olivewood brown, satin matt glaze

Lithium Carbonate	6.5
Zinc Oxide	17.6
Frit 25 (Pemco)	20.0
Kaolin	22.8
Flint	33.1
Add: Red Iron Oxide	2.0

GLAZE IX (Cone 4)
A buckskin brown, matt glaze

Whiting	16.8
Nepheline Syenite	38.8
Frit 54 (Pemco)	11.7
Kaolin	5.1
Flint	27.6
Add: Red Iron Oxide	5.0
Bentonite	2.0

GLAZE X (Cone 6 reduction)
A bright, celadon glaze

Volcanic Ash	83.4
Zinc Oxide	7.3
Whiting	9.3

GLAZE XI (Cone 6 reduction)
A bright, iron red glaze

Strontium Carbonate	3.0
Whiting	4.2
Zinc Oxide	9.7
Potash Feldspar	71.1
Kaolin	6.2
Flint	5.8
Add: Red Iron Oxide	13.0

GLAZE XII (Cone 9)
A sudan brown, matt glaze

Zinc Oxide	10.0
Albany Slip	85.0
Kaolin	5.0

GLAZE XIII (Cone 9 reduction)
An iron red glaze

Lithium Carbonate 2.2
Magnesium Carbonate 2.4
Whiting 16.4
Zinc Oxide 2.4
Potash Feldspar 24.8
Kaolin 10.0
Flint 41.8

Add: Red Iron Oxide 10.0

GLAZE XIV (Cone 10 reduction)
A bright, celadon glaze

Barium Carbonate 10.4
Lithium Carbonate 6.3
Strontium Carbonate 3.9
Whiting 9.2
Zinc Oxide 2.1
Potash Feldspar 21.6
Kaolin 10.1
Flint 36.4

Add: Red Iron Oxide 1.0

Chromium

Chromium found its place in formularies as a glaze colorant approximately 175 years ago. Its ability to produce a great variety of color has provided potters with many stable hues. Chromium will produce good green colors when added in amounts of one-half to one per cent to the average glaze free of compounds of tin, zinc, lead, barium, or titanium. Because of its limited solubility, green chrome oxide, when added to many glazes, may disperse and produce effects similar to insoluble pigments in enamels. Chrome oxide behaves chemically much like alumina so that some glazes must be used with a reduced alumina content to avoid too great a reduction of glaze viscosity at the maturing point.

During firing, highly volatile chrome oxide may cause susceptible glaze constituents like tin or titanium oxide to assume a pink color which is usually undesirable. This effect may migrate through the kiln atmosphere during firing to produce unwanted color in ware not otherwise influenced by chromium.

The warm and easily obtained coral red color produced by high lead glazes containing chrome oxide is a tempting color for the artist potter. Chrome coral red glazes though, should be used on decorative ware only, because of possible high lead release when they come in contact with acidic food.

Variations of chrome green glazes follow:

GLAZE XV (Cone 06)
An opaque, green glaze

Lithium Carbonate 7.8
Wollastonite 20.3
Frit 25 (Pemco) 47.2
Kaolin 18.7
Flint 6.0

Add: Chrome Oxide 0.8

GLAZE XVI (Cone 4)
A smooth, opaque, green glaze

Colemanite 49.4
Kaolin 15.6
Flint 35.0

Add: Chrome Oxide 1.0

GLAZE XVII (Cone 9)
A light green, stony matt glaze

Barium Carbonate 10.4
Magnesium Carbonate 2.7
Whiting 11.7
Nepheline Syenite 14.8
Frit 3134 (Ferro) 18.4
Flint 42.0

Add: Chrome Oxide 1.0

Cobalt

Compounds of cobalt are powerful colorants, resistant to changes in hue in various glazes, and resistant to changes in the kiln atmosphere. Cobalt compounds were used as ceramic colorants in Egypt as early as 5000 years ago. Zaffre, a cobalt silicate; and smalt, a cobalt glass, are examples of classic cobalt colorants used on historic ware.

Cobalt oxide (usually a mixture of cobalt compounds) is largely used to produce a blue color, while cobalt carbonate with sixty per cent of the tinting power of the black oxide, is used because of its good dispersion in glaze.

Colors other than blue may result when cobalt is added to glazes high in magnesium. Here is a short formulary of various cobalt colored glazes for the potter:

GLAZE XVIII (Cone 014)
A bright, blue glaze

Colemanite	27.5
Lithium Carbonate	7.8
Frit 25 (Pemco)	38.3
Kaolin	15.6
Flint	10.8

Add: Cobalt Carbonate 1.0

GLAZE XIX (Cone 06)
A clouded blue glaze

Gerstley Borate	65.5
Kaolin	9.3
Flint	25.2

Add: Cobalt Carbonate 1.0

GLAZE XX (Cone 4)
A satin matt, violet-toned glaze

Magnesium Carbonate	2.3
Wollastonite	23.0
Potash Feldspar	32.6
Flint	42.1

Add: Cobalt Carbonate 1.0

GLAZE XXI (Cone 4)
A bright, clouded blue glaze

Colemanite	42.8
Whiting	6.6
Potash Feldspar	34.6
Flint	16.0

Add: Cobalt Carbonate 1.0

GLAZE XXII (Cone 9)
A bright, blue glaze

Colemanite	23.9
Frit 25 (Pemco)	41.1
Kaolin	35.0

Add: Cobalt Carbonate 1.0

Manganese

Compounds of manganese have served as glaze colorants for the past two centuries, and produce an eggplant color in the more alkaline glazes, underglazes, and overglazes. Various commercial stains depend on the presence of manganese compounds to secure aubergine and dark colorations.

Because manganese colorants are relatively weak, a high percentage is sometimes used. Black manganese dioxide is often employed as a colorant, while manganese carbonate in a finely divided dried precipitate lends itself to smooth dispersion in the glaze. Manganese glazes can sometimes blister due to the liberation of volatile gases during the firing process.

GLAZE XXIII (Cone 04)
A smooth matt, brown glaze

Barium Carbonate	5.9
Lithium Carbonate	10.2
Whiting	9.8
Zinc Oxide	9.8
Kaolin	22.1
Flint	42.2

Add: Manganese Carbonate 3.0

GLAZE XXIV (Cone 3)
A bright, purple glaze

Lithium Carbonate	11.2
Sodium Silicofluoride	28.3
Kaolin	11.7
Flint	48.8

Add: Manganese Carbonate 3.0

GLAZE XXV (Cone 9)
A smooth matt, chocolate-colored glaze

Sodium Silicofluoride	9.1
Whiting	4.9
Kaolin	16.8
Calcined Kaolin	10.8
Flint	58.4

Add: Manganese Dioxide 19.8

Nickel

Nickel is a powerful colorant capable of coloring a glaze when present in only one part per fifty thousand. Depending on the composition of the glaze, nickel can produce gray, green, yellow-brown, icy blue, or rose red. Occasionally this colorant may change its degree of oxidation during firing, and blisters will roughen the glaze surface. Nickel's tendency to combine with silica, and crystallize, may also result in roughened glaze surfaces. Two oxides of nickel, one green, the other black, are often used as colorants. They differ in strength, but as marketed are more close in composition than is indicated by their formulas. Nickel carbonate is often favored since it disperses evenly in the glaze. Using from one-half to three per cent nickel can yield good color concentrations.

GLAZE XXVI (Cone 4)

Barium Carbonate 40.8
Lithium Carbonate 4.4
Zinc Oxide 11.0
Nepheline Syenite 24.6
Flint 19.2

Add: Bentonite 2.0
     Nickel Oxide 3.0

GLAZE XXVII (Cone 5)
A smooth matt, icy blue glaze

Barium Carbonate 15.8
Whiting 5.3
Zinc Oxide 12.1
Potash Feldspar 52.8
Kaolin 4.9
Flint 9.1

Add: Nickel Oxide 3.0

Stains

Ceramic stains are an extension of the hues made possible by colorants. They differ from the more simple oxides and carbonates by the preliminary processing which the stains undergo in preparation for their use in underglazes, glazes, and overglazes. The purpose of this processing is to render the colorants stable and consistent in use.

While stains may be successfully prepared by the potter, most of their production has been relegated to manufacturers who specialize in their involved formulation and purification. During the past thirty years, there has been much chemical research directed toward the production of a wider range of color and greater consistency in composition. Some recently developed stains are available in shades of vanadium-zirconium blue, indium orange, praesodymium yellow, and others. Complex research has established a broad temperature range in which these stains are effective. The artist-potter may find stain consistency and color difficult to secure with simple oxides and carbonates.

Making Frits

THE EXPERIMENTAL ARTIST-POTTER may often be confronted with the problem of developing a glaze to fit his varied needs. Each glaze ingredient has certain limitations — it must not be too soluble, nor produce faults in the fired glaze, nor be toxic to the user.

Frits, pre-fired and fused glaze materials, have provided the artist-potter with an alternative which frequently proves superior to the raw ceramic materials.

The knowledgeable ceramist, whether artist-potter or ceramic engineer, is turning increasingly to the use of frits as a main ingredient of glazes. By and large, frit is less likely to chemically attack underglaze colorants than are most raw glazes. The fritted glaze tends to fit the ware more evenly and yield more uniform colors, and the diminishing of gas evolution in the fritted glaze reduces the incidence of faults such as pinholing and blistering. The use of frits enables the potter to widen his glaze formulary through the use of metals such as sodium and potassium which are often unsuitable because of the need to carry an overload of alumina and silica when introduced in the raw glaze batch with feldspar. When toxic glaze materials such as soluble lead compounds must be included in glazes, incorporating these in frit may reduce risk of toxicity to the potter.

Although frits are generally more expensive than some of the raw materials when equated on a pound-to-pound basis, there is practically no loss of any part of the frit during a normal firing. Conversely, a loss of as much as forty per cent or more of some raw ingredients may occur. Thus, the actual cost of frit per unit of glaze is much reduced, and the more reliable performance of fritted glazes may alone justify their increased use.

While commercially available frits often serve the potter's needs, an artist-potter possessing the skills necessary to prepare a glaze may confidently undertake the preparation of a frit. The basic procedure for frit-making involves heating the materials in a thick-walled crucible, fragmenting the molten frit by pouring into cold water, and reducing it to a fine-mesh powder.

Crucibles suitable for melting metals are customarily stocked by chemical supply houses. They are satisfactory for frit-making purposes if they are first coated with a protective wash. This prevents the fireclay body of the crucible from imparting undesirable colorants to the frit during firing.

CRUCIBLE WASH
Use like kiln wash to coat and protect the inside of the crucible

Kaolin 70
Bentonite 3
Flint 27

For the potter who wishes to throw his own melting pot, a clay body is recommended as follows:

CRUCIBLE CLAY BODY
Kaolin 40
Calcined Kaolin 20
Tennessee Ball Clay (O.M.#1) 20
Grog 10
Flint 10

This clay body may be mixed dry and slaked with about 500 milliliters of water per 1,000 grams of dry mix. After an initial wetting period of about twenty-four hours, the moist clay should be allowed to mature for a week before being wedged and thrown. A preliminary firing of the thrown crucible to Cone 4 or higher is necessary before the pot can be successfully used for frit-making.

Commercially produced crucibles tend to be expensive; and since a crucible may be used only for the same frit formula to prevent contamination of the batch in subsequent preparations, the potter is well advised to throw his own containers. The size of the crucible is dependent on the amount of weight which the potter can handle comfortably when removing the liquid-filled pot from the kiln. A wall thickness approximately double that of an average pot should be adequate, and a pouring lip is needed.

Other basic equipment for frit preparation includes: a good pair of raku tongs, a metal bucket, and a porcelain mortar and pestle or a ball mill. A raku or glaze test kiln is convenient for firing.

One liter of ingredients provides about five pounds of frit. When the raw materials have been weighed out, they should be thoroughly mixed dry and passed through an 80- or 100-mesh sieve. The dry material is then packed into the crucible to about three-fourths its capacity so that any foaming during firing does not cause the molten frit to overflow.

When an inspection reveals that the initial fusion in the kiln has taken place, more raw mix can be added to the molten material, if desired, and the fusion carried to a point where a clear molten fluid is obtained.

At this point, the crucible of liquid frit is removed from the kiln with tongs and held about a foot above a metal bucket nearly filled with cold water. As the frit is poured into the water, it will fragment. The resultant product may be either ball-milled or ground wet in a porcelain mortar to a 100-mesh, or finer size. The ball mill will, of course, minimize the time and effort required. After drying, the frit may be used as a glaze ingredient or, with additions of suspending and adhesive agents, as a glaze.

In compounding a frit for varied uses, some simple guidelines should be observed to assure good fluidity and low solubility in water. Frits for general application are usually prepared from formulas involving major quantities of fluxing elements like sodium, potassium, lithium, lead, boron, and occasionally fluorine. The solubility of lead frits can be quite low provided the frit is properly balanced, and lead frits are considered as the safest form for the introduction of lead into a glaze. The alkaline metals, often kept below fifty per cent of the content of the frit, are most often included in the frit batch as carbonate, bicarbonate, or nitrate salts. The alkaline earths — calcium, barium, strontium, as well as zinc and magnesium — are all good frit stabilizers, and are customarily added as the carbonate form. Zinc is most often added in the oxide form. Boron, an extensively used fluxing ingredient in frits, is most frequently added as borax, boric acid, and occasionally as colemanite.

Alumina may be added to the frit formula in kaolin, or sometimes as alumina hydrate or simply as alumina. Most of the low-melting frits contain minimal levels of alumina in order to keep the melting point of the frit low. From 0.1 to 0.2 molar proportions of this oxide are considered adequate for use in a frit.

Silica is often incorporated in a frit formula as flint or may be partially supplied by a feldspar. It is common practice to hold the silica content to 1.5 to 3 molar equivalents.

Among some potters the preparation of specific frits may be extended to include a considerable variety of elements. Some of the special formulas produce frits which may be used alone as glazes. This rather ancient practice of forming frit glazes involves fritting together vegetable ash and silica. A more recent use is in the production of low temperature crystal or aventurine frit glazes.

FRIT I

Suitable for general use in low-melting glazes

Borax 39
Wollastonite 10
Potash Feldspar 33
Kaolin 4
Flint 14

FRIT II

Suitable for general use in low-melting glazes

Boric Acid 21
Potassium Nitrate 5
Soda Ash 26
Wollastonite 14
Kaolin 15
Flint 19

FRIT III

Suitable for use in viscous glazes

Borax 22
Soda Ash 13
Wollastonite 15
Potash Feldspar 17
Kaolin 11
Flint 22

FRIT IV

Suitable for use as a crystalline glaze at Cone 03 without further additions

Borax 14
Boric Acid 5
Copper Carbonate 1
Potassium Nitrate 7
Wollastonite 9
Zinc Oxide 27
Flint 37

Add: Bentonite 2

After fritting and grinding, apply as a glaze and fire to Cone 03, soak at Cone 03 for one hour, cool to Cone 010, soak at Cone 010 for three hours, then allow to cool normally.

FRIT V

A Seger frit suitable for use as a glaze at Cone 02 without further additions

Borax 45.5
Soda Ash 12.3
Whiting 23.2
Kaolin 12.0
Flint 7.0

Part II
A Glaze Formulary

Ash Glazes

ORGANIC ASH has served man for thousands of years as a prime source of alkaline chemicals, and has been used extensively as an essential material in the production of glazes.

Many potters of our time have utilized wood ash as a basic glaze ingredient in an effort to obtain textures and color which may be the result of the timing of the chemical reactions taking place in the glaze during firing. The ash resulting from the combustion of organic constituents is essentially in the form of mineral carbonates. Among these are the carbonates of potassium and calcium.

Ash may be quite different in composition from one organic species to another, as well as in the same species grown under different soil and climatic conditions. The amount and composition of the ash in the living parts may vary rather widely. In trees it may be said that:

1. More ash may be obtained from the limbs and branches than from the sap or heartwood.

2. The largest amount of ash may be obtained from the bark.

3. The most alkaline ash is to be found in fruit and husks.

4. Ash from the outside surfaces, as well as that from the fruit and husks, has the largest phosphorous oxide content.

5. Bark ash has the highest content of calcium oxide.

Comparatively little ash results from combustion. Tree ash yields may be as low as one-half pound per 100 pounds of wood. Most ash resulting from the combustion of plants contains significant amounts of calcium oxide, potash, sodium oxide, aluminum oxide, and silica along with smaller amounts of phosphorous oxide, iron oxide, and trace amounts of other elements, all of which exercise some influence on the glaze containing them. Under unusual conditions of growth, such as the presence of larger than normal amounts of minerals in the soil, ash may produce unexpected colorations or textures.

Ash recovered from trash burning may carry materials which are quite foreign to plant ash. Sites where sawmill waste or wood scraps are burned may yield good ash in large amounts. When considerable ash glazing is planned, fairly large quantities of ash should be stored to avoid replacement difficulties, and for continuing, consistent results. An initial processing of the ash with a

20-mesh screen, followed with proper mixing, are desirable steps.

It is common practice to leach the ash with water, although this is not mandatory. When the ash is added to water, much of the un-burned carbonaceous matter tends to float and can be skimmed off. Grit and sand tend to quickly settle and may be separated by pouring off the water that contains most of the ash in suspension. The settled, unwanted material is then discarded.

The water used in the initial leaching will contain much of the soluble potash and soda in the form of carbonates. By repeated soak-ings and settlement, practically all of the solu-ble alkaline material may be removed from the ash, and the remaining residue may then be dried for use. Ash may be used in the un-leached condition, although it may prove somewhat irritating to tender skin.

Firing temperatures most favored are in the stoneware range.

By establishing an arbitrary level of about fifty per cent ash in the glaze, formulas may be devised to meet the needs of various ranges of glaze maturation.

The following is a mix which might produce mature glazes at low temperatures when as much as fifty per cent ash is used in the glaze:

Boric Acid 33
Lithium Carbonate 32
Frit 25 (Pemco) 35

Add: Bentonite 2

A recipe for use with ash in the intermedi-ate firing ranges (Cone 4-6) is:

Lithium Carbonate 5
Nepheline Syenite 90
Kentucky Ball Clay (O.M. #4) 5

With ash additions, the following recipe may be fired at stoneware temperatures:

Barium Carbonate 8
Whiting 9
Potash Feldspar 58
Kaolin 20
Flint 5

Add: Bentonite 2

A synthetic ash may be prepared by using available materials, all of which carry small amounts of impurities found in natural ash:

SYNTHETIC ASH

Potash Feldspar 15.00
Whiting 60.00
Kentucky Ball Clay (O.M. #4) 9.00
Magnesium Carbonate 4.00
Bone Ash 7.00
Red Iron Oxide 0.50
Rutile 0.10
Fluorspar 0.10
Vanadium Oxide 0.05
Zircopax 0.05
Copper Oxide 0.05
Green Chromium Oxide 0.05
Zinc Oxide 0.10
Flint 4.00

Calcium in Glazes

CALCIUM IS ONE OF the most beneficial elements in ceramic glazes. The extensive use of calcium can be directly attributed to its many chemical properties and to the low cost of glaze materials containing calcium. With its strong affinity for combining with silica, calcium tends to form buffer layers between glaze and body, thus modifying the tension between them after firing. Calcium reduces crazing and shivering, hardens the glaze, and increases its resistance to weathering.

Excellent matt glazes are produced by calcium in excess amounts. In the presence of boric oxide, excess calcium tends to produce pleasant, waxy surfaces. When light or strong translucencies are desired, particularly with underglaze decoration, calcium may prove very satisfactory.

Calcium is most often added to a glaze as whiting ($CaCO_3$), a rather pure compound derived from natural deposits of limestone, chalk, or marble. It may also be obtained in a quite pure precipitated calcium carbonate.

Dolomite ($CaCO_3 \cdot MgCO_3$) is frequently used in glazes for its calcium content. In addition, many frits introduce considerable calcium into a glaze. Calcium phosphate [$Ca_3(PO_4)_2$], usually called bone ash; and fluorspar (CaF_2) are sometimes used in glaze formulas. Either may form a source of calcium in glazes.

Wollastonite ($CaO \cdot SiO_3$) has been more recently exploited for its calcium content, and it is of particular value for its frit-like character. Unlike whiting, it does not liberate large amounts of gas during firing. Pinholing and related defects are thus reduced with this mineral. Many potters currently use wollastonite for its potential to reduce firing shrinkage in clay bodies, when this silicate is substituted for whiting and flint in the formula. Many times it is added to a clay body along with pyrophyllite to produce flameware. In glazes, wollastonite has only a minimal tendency to produce color shifts during firing.

The following recipes containing high levels of calcium may be of interest to the potter:

GLAZE I (Cone 010)
A bright, somewhat opalescent glaze

Boric Acid 7.9
Frit 14 (Hommel) 81.1
Kaolin 11.0

GLAZE II (Cone 010)
A matt, almost stony glaze

Gerstley Borate 75.4
Wollastonite 6.5
Kaolin 11.2
Flint 6.9

GLAZE III (Cone 05)
A dense, opalescent glaze

Wollastonite 14.2
Frit 14 (Hommel) 34.5
Potash Feldspar 30.1
Kaolin 9.3
Flint 11.9

GLAZE IV (Cone 05)
A clear glaze

Gerstley Borate 61.4
Wollastonite 26.4
Kaolin 12.2

GLAZE V (Cone 4)
A satin matt glaze

Magnesium Carbonate 3.0
Wollastonite 22.7
Frit 14 (Hommel) 8.1
Potash Feldspar 28.1
Kaolin 17.0
Calcined Kaolin 15.0
Flint 6.1

GLAZE VI (Cone 4)
An opaque glaze

Barium Carbonate 7.1
Dolomite 6.9
Whiting 10.0
Zinc Oxide 8.9
Potash Feldspar 26.1
Kaolin 8.0
Zircopax 17.2
Flint 15.8

GLAZE VII (Cone 4)
A satin matt glaze

Magnesium Carbonate 2.8
Wollastonite 23.4
Frit 14 (Hommel) 11.1
Potash Feldspar 28.0
Kaolin 18.0
Calcined Kaolin 11.6
Flint 5.1

GLAZE VIII (Cone 4)
A clear glaze

Barium Carbonate 5.0
Dolomite 6.0
Whiting 11.0
Zinc Oxide 8.0
Potash Feldspar 28.0
Kaolin 15.0
Flint 27.0

GLAZE IX (Cone 4)
A clear, bright glaze

Magnesium Carbonate 2.7
Wollastonite 7.6
Zinc Oxide 4.1
Frit 14 (Hommel) 32.3
Potash Feldspar 9.4
Kaolin 17.5
Flint 26.4

GLAZE X (Cone 4)
A clear glaze

Gerstley Borate 50.0
Kaolin 15.0
Flint 35.0

GLAZE XI (Cone 9)
A satin matt glaze

Gerstley Borate 34.1
Kaolin 8.8
Calcined Kaolin 15.1
Flint 42.0

GLAZE XII (Cone 9)
A bright, opaque glaze

Wollastonite 22.7
Cryolite 12.1
Kaolin 14.9
Flint 50.3

GLAZE XIII (Cone 9)
A bright, clouded glaze

Magnesium Carbonate 1.5
Wollastonite 10.6
Frit 14 (Hommel) 12.1
Potash Feldspar 10.5
Kaolin 9.8
Calcined Kaolin 16.8
Flint 38.7

GLAZE XIV (Cone 9)
A satin matt glaze

Magnesium Carbonate 2.3
Wollastonite 23.0
Potash Feldspar 32.6
Flint 42.1

Cone 06 Fritted Glazes

A USEFUL FORMULARY of consistent low-temperature glazes may be compiled utilizing two synthetic frits, one natural frit (wollastonite), and ball clay.

Frit P-25 (Pemco) and Frit 14 (Hommel) contain an adequate balance of alkali metals and alkaline earths, as well as boric oxide, alumina, and some silica. When combined with a natural calcium silicate frit such as wollastonite, they form fairly stable glazes with a minimum inventory of materials. The incorporation of ball clay supplies the additional alumina necessary to obtain good stability, while also furnishing the adhesive qualities for the glaze.

Glazes prepared from these frit/clay combinations may be successfully colored with oxide and carbonate additives, and they respond well to opaquing and matting agents.

A saturated blue may be produced with the addition of one per cent cobalt oxide, while the incorporation of two per cent copper oxide may yield a turquoise blue. Shades of brown may be obtained with a five per cent addition of iron oxide or a four per cent addition of manganese dioxide. To achieve shades of green, one to three per cent of green chrome oxide may be included. A considerable variety of colors may be produced by five per cent additions of ceramic stains.

To opacify these fritted glazes, six per cent tin oxide or eight per cent Zircopax may be used. Incremental amounts (about five per cent each) of whiting or zinc oxide can be experimentally included to produce a matt effect in glazes not exhibiting that quality.

GLAZE I (Cone 06)
A matt glaze

Wollastonite 23
Frit 14 (Hommel) 57
Ball Clay 20

GLAZE II (Cone 06)
A matt glaze

Wollastonite 16
Frit 14 (Hommel) 55
Ball Clay 29

GLAZE III (Cone 06)
A stony matt glaze

Wollastonite 46
Frit 14 (Hommel) 26
Ball Clay 28

GLAZE IV (Cone 06)
A smooth matt glaze

Wollastonite	11
Frit 14 (Hommel)	38
Frit 25 (Pemco)	31
Ball Clay	20

GLAZE V (Cone 06)
A bright, slightly translucent glaze

Wollastonite	24
Frit 14 (Hommel)	20
Frit 25 (Pemco)	34
Ball Clay	22

GLAZE VI (Cone 06)
A translucent glaze

Wollastonite	20
Frit 25 (Pemco)	65
Ball Clay	15

GLAZE VII (Cone 06)
A translucent glaze

Wollastonite	10
Frit 14 (Hommel)	40
Frit 25 (Pemco)	35
Ball Clay	15

GLAZE VIII (Cone 06)
A bright, slightly translucent glaze

Wollastonite	18
Frit 25 (Pemco)	72
Ball Clay	10

GLAZE IX (Cone 06)
A bright, fissured glaze

Wollastonite	28
Frit 14 (Hommel)	20
Frit 25 (Pemco)	38
Ball Clay	14

GLAZE X (Cone 06)
A bright, translucent glaze

Wollastonite	20
Frit 25 (Pemco)	65
Ball Clay	15

GLAZE XI (Cone 06)
A smooth matt glaze

Wollastonite	25
Frit 14 (Hommel)	55
Ball Clay	20

GLAZE XII (Cone 06)
A bright, translucent glaze

Wollastonite	16
Frit 14 (Hommel)	38
Frit 25 (Pemco)	31
Ball Clay	15

GLAZE XIII (Cone 06)
A satin matt glaze

Wollastonite	40
Frit 14 (Hommel)	23
Ball Clay	37

GLAZE XIV (Cone 06)
A bright, translucent glaze

Wollastonite	25
Frit 14 (Hommel)	41
Ball Clay	34

GLAZE XV (Cone 06)
A bright, clear glaze

Wollastonite	12
Frit 14 (Hommel)	57
Ball Clay	31

GLAZE XVI (Cone 06)
A satin matt glaze

Wollastonite	20
Frit 25 (Pemco)	54
Ball Clay	26

GLAZE XVII (Cone 06)
A bright, translucent glaze

Wollastonite	8
Frit 25 (Pemco)	69
Ball Clay	23

GLAZE XVIII (Cone 06)
A bright, translucent glaze

Wollastonite	38
Frit 14 (Hommel)	11
Frit 25 (Pemco)	17
Ball Clay	34

GLAZE XIX (Cone 06)
A bright, clouded glaze

Wollastonite	22
Frit 14 (Hommel)	18
Frit 25 (Pemco)	32
Ball Clay	28

Cone 6 Oxidation Glazes

THERE ARE MANY ADVANTAGES TO Cone 6 glazes, and one of the most important of these is the color obtainable with various base formulas. Glazes fired to Cone 6 tend toward a broad spectrum — more complete than that possible with glazes fired to Cone 9 or 10, particularly in an oxidation atmosphere. The oxide and carbonate colorants added to Cone 6 glazes tend to break down and fade less than when fired to higher temperatures. As a class, stains are also quite useful at Cone 6.

As with glazes of all firing temperatures, the color of Cone 6 recipes is affected by certain elements contained in the glaze composition. Among them, zinc, calcium, and boron are commonly associated with affecting the action of glaze colorants, and fired glaze tests can readily show these tendencies.

A short formulary of Cone 6 oxidation recipes, prepared from a variety of fluxes, is appended below, and many of these will fire successfully between Cone 5 and 7, while all will give good results at Cone 6.

GLAZE I (Cone 6)
A matt glaze

Spodumene 53.0
Talc 44.8
Frit 14 (Hommel) 2.2

Add: Bentonite 2.0

GLAZE II (Cone 6)
A bright, translucent glaze

Lithium Carbonate 2.7
Strontium Carbonate 11.2
Zinc Oxide 7.7
Volcanic Ash 78.4

Add: Bentonite 2.0

GLAZE III (Cone 6)
A bright, slightly stony glaze

Whiting 1.6
Cryolite 8.4
Barnard Clay 90.0

Add: Bentonite 2.0

GLAZE IV (Cone 6)
A bright, light brown glaze

Cryolite 11.0
Albany Slip 89.0

Add: Bentonite 2.0

GLAZE V (Cone 6)
A bright, light brown, matt glaze

Wollastonite 9.8
Frit 14 (Hommel) 3.2
Albany Slip 87.0

Add: Bentonite 2.0

GLAZE VI (Cone 6)
A bright, mottled glaze

Lithium Carbonate 14.8
Albany Slip 74.2
Kaolin 11.0

Add: Bentonite 2.0

GLAZE VII (Cone 6)
A bright, matt glaze

Lithium Carbonate 0.9
Zinc Oxide 9.8
Kaolin 5.2
Albany Slip 84.1

GLAZE VIII (Cone 6)
A bright, clear glaze

Magnesium Carbonate 13.6
Zinc Oxide 12.9
Nepheline Syenite 35.4
Kaolin 2.5
Flint 35.6

GLAZE IX (Cone 6)
A bright, clouded glaze

Barium Carbonate 13.4
Lithium Carbonate 1.3
Magnesium Carbonate 1.3
Strontium Carbonate 5.0
Whiting 13.4
Potash Feldspar 37.2
Kaolin 4.3
Flint 24.1

GLAZE X (Cone 6)
A bright, opaque glaze

Lithium Carbonate 8.5
Magnesium Carbonate 9.0
Strontium Carbonate 14.3
Alumina Hydrate 5.0
Kaolin 16.7
Flint 46.5

GLAZE XI (Cone 6)
A satin matt glaze

Whiting 28.6
Potash Feldspar 39.7
Kaolin 13.8
Flint 17.9

GLAZE XII (Cone 6)
A satin matt glaze

Lithium Carbonate 1.6
Whiting 16.8
Zinc Oxide 17.8
Potash Feldspar 9.4
Kaolin 31.4
Flint 23.0

GLAZE XIII (Cone 6)
A smooth, mottled glaze

Lithium Carbonate 5.2
Whiting 3.5
Zinc Oxide 10.7
Potash Feldspar 49.2
Kaolin 15.4
Flint 16.0

GLAZE XIV (Cone 6)
A smooth, matt glaze

Lithium Carbonate 5.9
Whiting 6.0
Zinc Oxide 20.9
Kaolin 20.7
Titanium Dioxide 10.0
Flint 36.5

GLAZE XV (Cone 6)
A satin matt glaze

Strontium Carbonate 12.6
Zinc Oxide 25.8
Potash Feldspar 34.9
Kaolin 4.1
Flint 22.6

GLAZE XVI (Cone 6)
A mottled glaze

Lithium Carbonate 8.6
Strontium Carbonate 3.9
Zinc Oxide 18.7
Kaolin 21.1
Titanium Dioxide 6.2
Flint 41.5

GLAZE XVII (Cone 6)
A chocolate, matt glaze

Lithium Carbonate 10.7
Albany Slip 83.1
Rutile 6.2

Add: Bentonite 2.0

Cone 6 Reduction Glazes

IRON AND COPPER reduction glazes are considered to be among the most beautiful creations of the potter's art. These glazes have had a long existence since their first use by early Chinese potters. Today they are still highly respected. Successful and consistent reduction requires skill and experimentation in firing.

Following are recipes for several glazes with iron and copper pigmentation:

GLAZE I (Cone 6 reduction)
A satin, celadon glaze

Whiting	15.0
Zinc Oxide	12.0
Potash Feldspar	41.5
Kaolin	4.5
Flint	27.0
Add: Red Iron Oxide	1.0

GLAZE II (Cone 6 reduction)
A clouded, celadon glaze

Whiting	8.9
Zinc Oxide	8.4
Volcanic Ash	82.7

The colorant in this recipe is provided by the oxides naturally present in volcanic ash.

GLAZE III (Cone 6 reduction)
An iron red glaze

Strontium Carbonate	16.6
Zinc Oxide	9.7
Potash Feldspar	34.3
Kaolin	11.8
Flint	27.6
Add: Red Iron Oxide	13.0

The following copper red glazes were fired in oxidation to 1733°F (Cone 08), then in moderate reduction to 2194°F (Cone 6), at which point they were permitted to cool in the closed kiln.

GLAZE IV (Cone 6 reduction)
A bright, copper red glaze

Whiting	14.6
Frit 33 (Hommel)	27.0
Frit 3223 (Ferro)	11.4
Potash Feldspar	13.0
Kaolin	16.6
Flint	17.4
Add: Tin Oxide	1.0
Copper Carbonate	0.5

GLAZE V (Cone 6 reduction)
A copper red glaze

Dolomite	4.2
Whiting	6.9
Potash Feldspar	63.0
Kaolin	5.9
Flint	20.0
Add: Tin Oxide	1.0
Copper Carbonate	0.5

Cone 8 Stoneware Glazes

WITH THE DEVELOPMENT of the enclosed kiln in ancient China, it became possible for the potter to fire stoneware. Archaeological finds suggest that as early as 1500 B.C., glazed proto-porcelain was produced at temperatures near 2400°F but there is still much mystery surrounding this early era. We know, however, that after a long period of earthenware production, glazed Chinese stoneware was regularly produced by the end of the Han dynasty (206 B.C. — 200 A.D.).

European stoneware appeared much later, perhaps as early as the 12th century. Salt-glazed stoneware, developed in the 15th century by Rhineland potters, eventually spread to North America where it was a substantial part of the traditional folk potter's production.

Over the past fifty years, technological developments have placed the stoneware firing temperatures within the practical reach of nearly every contemporary ceramic artist. Advances in metallurgical research produced electrical heating elements which enabled the amateur as well as the professional potter to purchase various mobile kilns with the potential for attaining the higher firing ranges.

While most studio stoneware firings have traditionally been in the Cone 9-10 range, lower firing temperatures may also be considered such as Cone 8. At this temperature, the conventional oxide and carbonate colorants as well as the extensive number of stains may retain more color, while the stresses of higher firing temperatures and time of firing are reduced.

A Cone 8 formulary which may be fired both in oxidation and in reduction may prove useful to the potter:

GLAZE I (Cone 8)
A bright, translucent glaze

Whiting	9.1
Zinc Oxide	9.7
Potash Feldspar	50.5
Kaolin	18.0
Flint	12.7

GLAZE II (Cone 8)
A bright, translucent glaze

Whiting 7.4
Potash Feldspar 65.6
Kaolin 15.2
Flint 11.8

GLAZE III (Cone 8)
A bright, clear glaze

Magnesium Carbonate 2.2
Whiting 18.1
Potash Feldspar 29.0
Kaolin 16.7
Flint 34.0

GLAZE IV (Cone 8)
A dry matt glaze

Magnesium Carbonate 2.0
Whiting 11.7
Potash Feldspar 13.0
Alumina Hydrate 10.9
Kaolin 12.0
Flint 50.4

GLAZE V (Cone 8)
A cratered glaze

Gerstley Borate 6.1
Potash Feldspar 65.6
Flint 28.3

Add: Bentonite 2.0

Glaze VI (Cone 8)
A bright, translucent glaze

Magnesium Carbonate 2.0
Whiting 18.0
Frit 14 (Hommel) 10.0
Nepheline Syenite 21.0
Kaolin 24.0
Flint 25.0

GLAZE VII (Cone 8)
A bright glaze with small craters

Talc 13.8
Whiting 10.6
Potash Feldspar 53.2
Kaolin 3.2
Flint 19.2

GLAZE VIII (Cone 8)
A translucent, deep brown glaze

Cryolite 10.0
Albany Slip 90.0

GLAZE IX (Cone 8)
A translucent, deep brown glaze

Wollastonite 10.0
Albany Slip 90.0

GLAZE X (Cone 8)
A cratered, red-brown glaze

Fluorspar 4.0
Lithium Carbonate 2.0
Wollastonite 13.1
Frit 14 (Hommel) 6.1
Barnard Slip 50.6
Flint 24.2

Add: Bentonite 2.0

GLAZE XI (Cone 8)
A translucent glaze

Magnesium Carbonate 3.0
Whiting 16.8
Potash Feldspar 47.5
Kaolin 5.0
Flint 27.7

Add: Bentonite 2.0

GLAZE XII (Cone 8)
A bright, translucent glaze

Gerstley Borate 23.2
Frit 25 (Pemco) 14.7
Potash Feldspar 20.0
Kaolin 12.6
Flint 29.5

GLAZE XIII (Cone 8)
A bright, clear glaze

Whiting 19.0
Lepidolite 48.0
Flint 33.0

Add: Bentonite 2.0

GLAZE XIV (Cone 8)
A translucent glaze

Magnesium Carbonate 1.7
Whiting 10.4
Potash Feldspar 57.9
Flint 30.0

Add: Bentonite 2.0

GLAZE XV (Cone 8)
A matt, medium yellow glaze

Gerstley Borate 22.4
Kaolin 8.2
Volcanic Ash 40.8
Flint 28.6

GLAZE XVI (Cone 8)
A fissured, dark yellow glaze

Spodumene 10.0
Albany Slip 80.0
Kentucky Ball Clay 10.0

GLAZE XVII (Cone 8)
A glossy, patterned glaze

Whiting 15.1
Frit 14 (Hommel) 23.9
Kaolin 28.7
Titanium Dioxide 9.6
Flint 22.7

GLAZE XVIII (Cone 8)
A bright, patterned glaze

Talc 35.1
Whiting 11.7
Nepheline Syenite 24.5
Kaolin 18.1
Titanium Dioxide 10.6

GLAZE XIX (Cone 8)
A red-black glaze

Lithium Carbonate 25.0
Barnard Slip 75.0

GLAZE XX (Cone 8)
A bright, red-black glaze

Whiting 10.0
Barnard Slip 90.0

GLAZE XXI (Cone 8)
A glossy, red-black glaze

Gerstley Borate 4.0
Barnard Slip 96.0

GLAZE XXII (Cone 8)
A transparent, yellow-brown glaze

Whiting 12.0
Zinc Oxide 12.0
Potash Feldspar 35.0
Red Clay 20.0
Flint 21.0

GLAZE XXIII (Cone 8)
A matt, red-brown glaze

Whiting 5.0
Red Clay 95.0

Cone 10 Reduction Glazes

GLAZES AND CLAY BODIES fired under reducing conditions have long offered the artist-potter warm color and textural values.

These characteristics are the result of the reducing chemical reactions which occur during the formation of the glaze in the firing process. The excess carbon monoxide gas in the kiln atmosphere during the reduction period tempers and changes glaze and body colors, and glaze texture. These Cone 10 reduction formulas may provide a few additions to the artist-potter's formulary:

GLAZE I (Cone 10 reduction)
A smooth matt glaze

Magnesium Carbonate 1.9
Whiting 16.4
Spodumene 17.3
Kaolin 12.1
Calcined Kaolin 8.3
Flint 44.0

GLAZE II (Cone 10 reduction)
A bright, opaque, murky glaze

Boron Phosphate 6.6
Whiting 17.1
Potash Feldspar 40.6
Kaolin 6.6
Flint 29.1

GLAZE III (Cone 10 reduction)
A bright, semiopaque glaze which may be mottled

Lithium Carbonate 3.3
Whiting 6.8
Volcanic Ash 89.9

Add: Bentonite 2.0

GLAZE IV (Cone 10 reduction)
A bright, semiopaque glaze

Whiting 19.3
Spodumene 30.7
Kaolin 7.1
Flint 42.9

GLAZE V (Cone 10 reduction)
A bright, mottled glaze

Boric Acid 1.6
Sodium Silicofluoride 15.1
Portland Cement 24.5
Kaolin 13.8
Flint 45.0

GLAZE VI (Cone 10 reduction)
A bright, opaque, mottled glaze

Lithium Carbonate 3.3
Whiting 6.6
Kaolin 2.8
Volcanic Ash 87.3

GLAZE VII (Cone 10 reduction)
A bright, opaque, mottled glaze

Whiting 10.5
Zinc Oxide 4.2
Cryolite 16.6
Kaolin 13.6
Flint 55.1

GLAZE VIII (Cone 10 reduction)
A satin matt glaze

Magnesium Carbonate 8.5
Wollastonite 29.0
Calcined Kaolin 7.8
Kaolin 18.3
Flint 36.4

GLAZE IX (Cone 10 reduction)
A bright, opaque, mottled glaze

Gerstley Borate 20.2
Kaolin 9.2
Volcanic Ash 41.1
Flint 29.5

GLAZE X (Cone 10 reduction)
A mottled, matt glaze for single firing

Gerstley Borate 13.5
Lithium Carbonate 26.5
Tennessee Ball Clay #1 . . . . 60.0

Crater Glazes

CRATER GLAZES, sometimes designated as lava or blister glazes, may be used to achieve textural emphasis on ware. Such glazes are usually produced by glaze compositions which liberate a gas during firing. As the gas bubbles reach the surface of the glaze, they may either break through to leave craters in the surface coating, or they may be trapped in the form of blisters. The principal factors determining the size and character of the crater effect are: the rate of firing, the temperature, and the viscosity of the glaze at the point of maturity.

Various granular chemicals or minerals can be included in a glaze formula (in amounts of one or two per cent) to serve as bubble producers. At stoneware levels, granular gypsum may yield sulphurous gases, while granular manganese dioxide, silicon carbide, or magnesium carbonate can liberate carbon dioxide or oxygen at earthenware temperatures. As a simple means of preparing a granular form of gypsum, a ¼-inch layer of plaster of Paris (a form of gypsum) can be cast on cloth. When set, the material may be easily crushed with a roller and screened to a desirable particle size. The crushed plaster is first passed through a 60-mesh screen, then any material which will not pass through an 80-mesh screen is retained. Small amounts of 50- to 100-mesh silicon carbide may also be used experimentally.

Generally, the rates of firing and cooling are on the rapid side. The potter will probably achieve best control when the progress of the firing is closely monitored through a peephole. If the glaze is overfired, the surface may tend to heal over and obliterate the desired crater effects. Several experimental firings will be needed to determine the conditions which will yield repeatable results in a given kiln.

Producing the crater glaze is somewhat subjective on the part of the potter, and it may seem difficult to break with traditional efforts to produce "good" glazes and strive for faulting. The potential, however, for obtaining textural variety on ware should justify the effort. A selection of glaze formulas which produce various crater effects may provide some guidance for the potter who wishes to experiment with this technique.

GLAZE I (Cone 015)

Lithium Carbonate 11.0
Sodium Silicofluoride 28.0
Alumina Hydrate 16.3
Flint 44.7

Add: Bentonite 1.0

GLAZE II (Cone 06)

Sodium Silicofluoride 42.7
Whiting 15.2
Kaolin 19.3
Flint 22.8

GLAZE III (Cone 04)
Fluorspar 3.9
Magnesium Carbonate 2.9
Cryolite 9.8
Kaolin 11.8
Flint 71.6

GLAZE IV (Cone 1)
Whiting 19.6
Frit 14 (Hommel) 29.4
Nepheline Syenite 49.0
Silicon Carbide (Granular) 2.0

Add: Bentonite 1.0

GLAZE V (Cone 4)
Fluorspar 19.0
Cryolite 34.3
Kaolin 9.0
Flint 37.7

GLAZE VI (Cone 4)
Zinc Oxide 11.8
Potash Feldspar 74.5
Kaolin 13.7

GLAZE VII (Cone 4)
Fluorspar 12.6
Sodium Silicofluoride 4.9
Lepidolite 50.5
Flint 32.0

GLAZE VIII (Cone 4)
Fluorspar 15.2
Magnesium Carbonate 2.9
Zinc Oxide 4.4
Cryolite 10.2
Kaolin 14.0
Flint 53.3

GLAZE IX (Cone 4)
Fluorspar 12.4
Sodium Fluoride 2.8
Lepidolite 52.0
Flint 32.8

GLAZE X (Cone 4)
Fluorspar 14.6
Cryolite 26.3
Kaolin 21.0
Flint 38.1

GLAZE XI (Cone 4)
Talc 50.0
Cryolite 50.0

Add: Bentonite 2.0

GLAZE XII (Cone 4)
Bone Ash 30.0
Frit 25 (Pemco) 55.0
Kaolin 15.0

GLAZE XIII (Cone 4)
Fluorspar 19.0
Cryolite 34.3
Kaolin 9.0
Flint 37.7

GLAZE XIV (Cone 4)
Fluorspar 6.3
Magnesium Carbonate 1.2
Zinc Oxide 1.6
Cryolite 41.8
Kaolin 5.7
Flint 43.4

Glazes for Infrequently Used Cone Levels

GLAZE FIRINGS tend to be limited to a few basic cone levels because of local, national, or international custom. At times the potter may find reason to deviate from such patterns of firing as a method of adjusting the qualities of a recipe or for the sake of experiment. Fortunately, most glazes have a range of useful cone levels throughout which they can produce very similar results.

The successful firing of any glaze batch is subject to a number of influences. Among these is the composition of the batch (which to a large degree determines the "fit" between glaze and clay body), the method of firing, the rate of temperature climb, and glaze application. Variations in these influences sometimes suggest a change in cone level. The potter may wish to fire familiar recipes to determine the effects of one or more of the less frequently used cone levels; or, he may wish to experiment with the following glaze recipes:

GLAZE I (Cone 020)
A clear glaze

Gerstley Borate	34.3
Lithium Carbonate	9.0
Frit 25 (Pemco)	53.1
Kaolin	3.6

GLAZE II (Cone 020)
A clear glaze

Gerstley Borate	40.0
Lithium Carbonate	5.0
Cryolite	10.0
Frit 25 (Pemco)	25.0
Flint	20.0

GLAZE III (Cone 018)
A clear glaze

Lithium Carbonate	10.1
Frit 259 (Hommel)	44.1
Frit 14 (Hommel)	25.7
Kaolin	5.9
Flint	14.2

GLAZE IV (Cone 015)
A clear glaze

Gerstley Borate	38.4
Frit 25 (Pemco)	57.7
Kaolin	3.9

GLAZE V (Cone 012)
A translucent glaze

Lithium Carbonate	9.7
Frit 25 (Pemco)	39.8
Frit 54 (Pemco)	23.9
Kaolin	10.7
Flint	15.9

GLAZE VI (Cone 012)
A translucent glaze

Sodium Silicofluoride	5.3
Frit 14 (Hommel)	74.0
Kaolin	4.7
Flint	16.0

GLAZE VII (Cone 09)
A translucent glaze

Gerstley Borate	69.3
Magnesium Carbonate	17.7
Frit 3134 (Ferro)	12.0
Kaolin	1.0

GLAZE VIII (Cone 09)
A translucent glaze

Gerstley Borate	17.8
Whiting	11.3
Frit 25 (Pemco)	51.5
Flint	19.4
Add: Bentonite	2.0

GLAZE IX (Cone 09)
A translucent glaze

Gerstley Borate	88.5
Whiting	4.3
Kaolin	7.2

GLAZE X (Cone 08)
A bright, opaque glaze

Gerstley Borate 7.6
Strontium Carbonate 21.8
Whiting 2.9
Frit 25 (Pemco) 28.2
Kaolin 6.0
Flint 33.5

GLAZE XI (Cone 08)
A translucent glaze

Gerstley Borate 26.6
Strontium Carbonate 15.1
Frit 25 (Pemco) 32.5
Flint 25.8

Add: Bentonite 2.0

GLAZE XII (Cone 08)
A bright, matt glaze

Whiting 13.1
Zinc Oxide 10.9
Frit 25 (Pemco) 38.9
Flint 37.1
Add: Bentonite 2.0

GLAZE XIII (Cone 08)
A bright, matt glaze

Lithium Carbonate 3.9
Frit 25 (Pemco) 33.8
Frit 54 (Pemco) 39.2
Flint 23.1
Add: Bentonite 2.0

GLAZE XIV (Cone 07)
A translucent glaze

Barium Carbonate 2.6
Whiting 5.6
Frit 3269 (Ferro) 44.1
Nepheline Syenite 12.4
Kaolin 10.5
Flint 24.8

GLAZE XV (Cone 07)
A translucent glaze

Gerstley Borate 35.8
Zinc Oxide 6.0
Frit 3269 (Ferro) 21.1
Kaolin 10.8
Flint 26.3

GLAZE XVI (Cone 03)
A clear glaze

Gerstley Borate 6.4
Whiting 9.8
Frit 3269 (Ferro) 38.8
Alumina Hydrate 4.6
Kaolin 12.6
Flint 27.8

GLAZE XVII (Cone 03)
A matt glaze

Lithium Carbonate 1.8
Whiting 4.8
Zinc Oxide 26.8
Nepheline Syenite 32.1
Flint 34.5

Add: Bentonite 2.0

GLAZE XVIII (Cone 02)
A translucent glaze

Whiting 18.2
Zinc Oxide 3.0
Frit 25 (Pemco) 24.2
Kaolin 15.2
Flint 39.4

GLAZE XIX (Cone 02)
A translucent glaze

Gerstley Borate 35.6
Zinc Oxide 5.9
Frit 25 (Pemco) 20.7
Kaolin 10.8
Flint 27.0

GLAZE XX (Cone 01)
A satin matt glaze

Whiting 18.3
Frit 14 (Hommel) 12.3
Nepheline Syenite 69.4

Add: Bentonite 2.0

GLAZE XXI (Cone 01)
A matt glaze

Lithium Carbonate 2.0
Whiting 5.4
Zinc Oxide 30.4
Potash Feldspar 45.4
Kaolin 7.0
Flint 9.8

GLAZE XXII (Cone 1)
A semimatt glaze

Barium Carbonate	4.9
Gerstley Borate	19.3
Magnesium Carbonate	2.0
Whiting	29.6
Potash Feldspar	19.1
Flint	25.1
Add: Bentonite	2.0

GLAZE XXIII (Cone 2)
A bright, matt glaze

Barium Carbonate	6.9
Whiting	9.8
Zinc Oxide	10.5
Potash Feldspar	72.8
Add: Bentonite	2.0

GLAZE XXIV (Cone 2)
A satin matt glaze

Lithium Carbonate	1.6
Whiting	37.8
Zinc Oxide	6.4
Kaolin	37.8
Flint	16.4

GLAZE XXV (Cone 3)
A translucent glaze

Gerstley Borate	9.5
Whiting	9.5
Frit 25 (Pemco)	38.1
Alumina Hydrate	7.0
Kaolin	12.7
Flint	23.2

GLAZE XXVI (Cone 3)
A satin matt glaze

Barium Carbonate	28.8
Magnesium Carbonate	13.0
Whiting	8.1
Potash Feldspar	30.6
Flint	19.5
Add: Bentonite	2.0

GLAZE XXVII (Cone 4)
A satin matt glaze

Magnesium Carbonate	2.3
Wollastonite	23.0
Potash Feldspar	32.6
Flint	42.1
Add: Bentonite	2.0

GLAZE XXVIII (Cone 4)
A matt glaze

Strontium Carbonate	16.6
Zinc Oxide	9.7
Potash Feldspar	34.1
Kaolin	11.8
Flint	27.8

GLAZE XXIX (Cone 4)
A matt glaze

Whiting	10.6
Wollastonite	13.9
Zinc Oxide	10.2
Potash Feldspar	47.2
Kaolin	18.1

GLAZE XXX (Cone 5)
A satin matt glaze

Magnesium Carbonate	2.7
Wollastonite	22.6
Frit 54 (Pemco)	10.7
Potash Feldspar	28.0
Kaolin	18.7
Calcined Kaolin	11.8
Flint	5.5

GLAZE XXXI (Cone 5)
An opaque glaze

Lithium Carbonate	9.8
Magnesium Carbonate	10.1
Whiting	10.5
Kaolin	16.8
Calcined Kaolin	7.1
Flint	45.7

GLAZE XXXII (Cone 7)
A bright, opaque glaze

Gerstley Borate	50.3
Alumina Hydrate	3.8
Kaolin	10.0
Flint	35.9

High Magnesia Glazes for Cone 6

MAGNESIA is a common ingredient in many ceramic glazes, and its presence, even in small amounts, may add materially to their physical, chemical, and aesthetic qualities. In amounts up to 0.3 equivalents, it strengthens and hardens the glaze, thus enabling it to withstand wear and weathering. It is an effective matting agent and can contribute much to the "feel" of a glaze, particularly if fired in reduction.

When magnesia is present in excess of 0.3 molecular equivalents it has a tendency to render the glaze stony and dry, a desirable quality suited to some ceramic pieces. Magnesia also can serve as an effective flux when used as a major glaze constituent and fired at Cone 6 or above.

Magnesia can be introduced into the glaze as magnesium carbonate, or it may be introduced as an impurity in other glaze materials.

Many formularies include magnesia in their glazes, but few recipes are available in which the magnesia is present in amounts of about 0.4 molal equivalents. A number of these, all maturing at Cone 6 are offered here.

GLAZE I (Cone 6)
A semistony glaze

Lithium Carbonate 9.0
Magnesium Carbonate 10.0
Whiting 10.3
Kaolin 17.8
Calcined Kaolin 7.6
Flint 45.3

GLAZE II (Cone 6)
A stony glaze

Lithium Carbonate 23.6
Magnesium Carbonate 17.8
Kaolin 20.5
Flint 38.1

GLAZE III (Cone 6)
A dense, stony glaze

Talc 45.5
Spodumene 54.5

GLAZE IV (Cone 6)
A clear, bright glaze

Gerstley Borate 12.6
Magnesium Carbonate 10.3
Zinc Oxide 5.0
Nepheline Syenite 28.2
Kaolin 8.1
Flint 35.8

GLAZE V (Cone 6)
A clear, bright glaze

Magnesium Carbonate 13.6
Zinc Oxide 12.9
Nepheline Syenite 35.4
Kaolin 2.5
Flint 35.6

Oxidation Glazes for Cone 7

OXIDATION GLAZES, fired to Cone 7, can produce effects typical of the stoneware range, but with potential savings in reduced kiln wear and electrical consumption for those usually firing at higher temperatures. While not a typical cone range, Cone 7 may produce vitrified ware and significant glaze effects. The following formulary is designed for the potter firing an oxidation atmosphere:

GLAZE I (Cone 7)
A bright, opaque glaze

Lithium Carbonate	3.2
Magnesium Carbonate	2.0
Whiting	16.8
Frit 3134 (Ferro)	8.8
Kaolin	14.4
Calcined Kaolin	12.4
Flint	42.4

GLAZE II (Cone 7)
A bright, clouded glaze

Gerstley Borate	47.0
Kaolin	12.8
Calcined Kaolin	6.8
Flint	33.4

GLAZE III (Cone 7)
A bright glaze

Lithium Carbonate	3.4
Whiting	4.5
Zinc Oxide	10.7
Potash Feldspar	49.2
Kaolin	16.1
Flint	16.1

GLAZE IV (Cone 7)
A bright, crackled glaze

Barium Carbonate	13.0
Magnesium Carbonate	1.3
Strontium Carbonate	4.8
Whiting	13.0
Zinc Oxide	1.3
Nepheline Syenite	29.2
Kaolin	4.2
Flint	33.2

GLAZE V (Cone 7)
A matt glaze

Lithium Carbonate	9.0
Magnesium Carbonate	10.0
Whiting	10.3
Kaolin	17.8
Calcined Kaolin	7.6
Flint	45.3

GLAZE VI (Cone 7)
A bright, cordovan brown glaze

Albany Slip	77
Kaolin	8
Manganese Dioxide	15

GLAZE VII (Cone 7)
A bright, black glaze

Potash Feldspar	3
Albany Slip	90
Cobalt Oxide	1
Manganese Dioxide	2
Green Chromium Oxide	2
Red Iron Oxide	2

GLAZE VIII (Cone 7)
A stony matt glaze

Zinc Oxide	12
Potash Feldspar	75
Kaolin	13

GLAZE IX (Cone 7)
A rugged black glaze

Cryolite	10
Barnard Clay	90
Add: Bentonite	2

GLAZE X (Cone 7)
A patterned glaze

Fluorspar	4.8
Lithium Carbonate	2.2
Wollastonite	12.6
Frit 14 (Hommel)	6.0
Barnard Clay	50.2
Flint	24.2
Add: Bentonite	2.0

Simple Fritted Glazes

GLAZES WITH LARGE proportions of frit are usually more simple to prepare and fire than those made from unfritted raw materials.

Many different commercial frits are offered by manufacturers. One of these, much used by artist-potters, is known by three different trade names — Ferro frit 3134, Hommel frit 14, or Pemco frit 54. Calcium, sodium, and boron oxides are combined with silica in this frit whose proportions are favorable to the production of stable glazes, with the addition of pyrophyllite ($Al_2O_3 \cdot 4SiO_2 \cdot H_2O$), or kaolin. Such combinations of glaze materials tend to provide a wide range of firing temperatures. When kaolin is selected for the following glaze recipes, calcined kaolin is used to avoid cracking of the drying glaze. If raw kaolin is heated in the kiln to Cone 06 or more, it is converted into the calcined variety. Bentonite is added to prevent settling of the glaze.

GLAZE I (Cone 06)
A crackled clear glaze

Frit 3134 (Ferro) 89
Calcined Kaolin 11

Add: Bentonite 2

GLAZE II (Cone 06)
A lightly opaqued glaze

Frit 3134 (Ferro) 63
Calcined Kaolin 37

Add: Bentonite 2

GLAZE III (Cone 1)
An opaque glaze

Frit 3134 (Ferro) 77
Calcined Kaolin 23

Add: Bentonite 2

GLAZE IV (Cone 1)
An opaque glaze

Frit 3134 (Ferro) 62
Pyrophyllite 38

Add: Bentonite 2

GLAZE V (Cone 4)
A clear glaze

Frit 3134 (Ferro) 74
Calcined Kaolin 26

Add: Bentonite 2

GLAZE VI (Cone 4)
An opaque glaze

Frit 3134 (Ferro) 52
Pyrophyllite 48

Add: Bentonite 2

GLAZE VII (Cone 9)
A clear glaze

Frit 3134 (Ferro) 25
Pyrophyllite 75

Add: Bentonite 2

GLAZE VIII (Cone 9)
A clear glaze

Frit 3134 (Ferro) 64
Calcined Kaolin 36

Add: Bentonite 2

GLAZE IX (Cone 9)
An opaque glaze

Frit 3134 (Ferro) 35
Pyrophyllite 65

Add: Bentonite 2

Single-Fire Glazes

SINGLE FIRING may be considered the original ceramic technique from which bisque firing has evolved. The popularity of two firings for studio production can be partially attributed to diminished breakage when handling the more durable bisqued ware.

Modern technology has solved many of the problems inherent in single firing, a practice which is common in industry. The need in industry to conserve energy, cut labor costs, and reduce kiln replacement may parallel the needs of the potter and induce him to adopt the skills required to glaze greenware.

Most clay bodies now being used by the studio potter may be successfully single fired. When prepared with a major portion of plastic clays, the pore size of greenware is reduced, impeding glaze-water penetration. Using plastic clay bodies may result in improved green strength. Organic binders can be used to improve body strength, but they require a firing to burn out combustible materials with-out disturbing the glaze. A better solution is the addition before slaking of one and one-half per cent bentonite.

Greenware should be thoroughly dried prior to glazing to gain its maximum strength. If part of the ware retains water, it may slump or crack after glaze is applied. The exceptions are protrudent or thin sections of the ware which should be lightly moistened, perhaps by draping a damp cloth on them immediately before glazing. This avoids the sudden strain which may result in cracking when a large volume of wet glaze surrounds more-fragile parts of the ware. Very thin-walled ware requires extra care during single-fire glazing.

If the exterior of a pot has been glazed, it is often expedient to allow a period of drying before the inside coat is applied.

When fired slowly, glaze recipes designed for bisque will often work well on greenware. During the firing, greenware shrinks much more than bisque, and glazes with large amounts of clay follow the shrinkage rate of the green body more closely, reducing the chance of glaze faults.

Thicker glazes are important for single firing, and glaze density may be recorded with an inexpensive hydrometer (available from ceramics supply companies). An approximate specific gravity of 1.6 is suitable.

Glazes will tend to "fit" better if they contain significant amounts of calcium (as found in whiting, for example). Whiting tends to promote clay/glaze interlayer bonding, and about five per cent whiting will sometimes be effective when added to the body.

Slow firing of the glazed greenware should approximate bisque firing to assure proper maturing of the body and a desirable glaze reaction.

A formulary of glazes used successfully on greenware will demonstrate some of the possibilities for the potter:

GLAZE I (Cone 06)
A satin matt glaze

Whiting 10.7
Lithium Carbonate 6.0
Sodium Fluosilicate 15.3
Ball Clay 13.3
Flint 54.7

GLAZE II (Cone 06)
A clear glaze

Sodium Fluosilicate 35.6
Frit 14 (Hommel) 36.0
Ball Clay 20.3
Flint 8.1

GLAZE III (Cone 1)
A clear glaze

Frit 14 (Hommel) 60.0
Ball Clay 20.0
Kaolin 20.0

GLAZE IV (Cone 1)
A bright, matt glaze

Lithium Carbonate 11.8
Sodium Fluosilicate 11.8
Zinc Oxide 11.8
Albany Slip 17.6
Ball Clay 47.0

GLAZE V (Cone 1)
A bright, matt glaze

Lithium Carbonate 1.2
Magnesium Carbonate 2.6
Whiting 11.3
Frit 14 (Hommel) 30.8
Ball Clay 25.0
Flint 29.1

GLAZE VI (Cone 1)
A bright, semitranslucent glaze

Lithium Carbonate 2.2
Magnesium Carbonate 2.4
Whiting 15.0
Frit 14 (Hommel) 40.9
Ball Clay 34.8
Flint 4.7

GLAZE VII (Cone 1)
A satin matt glaze

Lithium Carbonate 2.2
Magnesium Carbonate 2.4
Whiting 17.8
Potash Feldspar 32.8
Ball Clay 30.6
Flint 14.2

GLAZE VIII (Cone 4)
A clear glaze

Magnesium Carbonate 3.0
Whiting 2.0
Frit 14 (Hommel) 14.9
Potash Feldspar 28.7
Ball Clay 26.7
Flint 24.7

GLAZE IX (Cone 4)
A bright, satin matt, "old gold" glaze

Lithium Carbonate 8.9
Albany Slip 78.9
Opax 12.2

GLAZE X (Cone 4)
A satin matt glaze

Gerstley Borate 50.0
Ball Clay 50.0

GLAZE XI (Cone 4)
A bright yellow, clear glaze

Gerstley Borate 50.0
Barnard Slip 25.0
Ball Clay 25.0

GLAZE XII (Cone 4)
A bright, clear glaze

Gerstley Borate 50.0
Albany Slip 25.0
Ball Clay 25.0

GLAZE XIII (Cone 4)
A rugged-surface glaze

Sodium Fluosilicate 22.2
Ball Clay 55.6
Volcanic Ash 22.2

GLAZE XIV (Cone 4)
A dry, bright-surfaced glaze

Sodium Fluosilicate 15.0
Whiting 45.0
Ball Clay 40.0

GLAZE XV (Cone 9 oxidation or reduction)
A bright matt glaze

Gerstley Borate 15.0
Lithium Carbonate 30.0
Ball Clay 55.0

GLAZE XVI (Cone 9 oxidation or reduction)
A stony matt glaze

Barium Carbonate 17.5
Gerstley Borate 20.0
Ball Clay 62.5

GLAZE XVII (Cone 9 oxidation or reduction)
A chocolate brown, opaque glaze

Gerstley Borate 20.0
Barnard Slip 50.0
Ball Clay 30.0

GLAZE XVIII (Cone 9 oxidation or reduction)
A stony matt glaze

Barium Carbonate 33.6
Gerstley Borate 11.4
Ball Clay 55.0

GLAZE XIX (Cone 9 oxidation or reduction)
A bright, stony matt glaze

Gerstley Borate 13.0
Whiting 34.8
Ball Clay 52.2

Tin in Glazes

TIN IS PRIMARILY an opaquing agent, but it also helps to reduce crazing tendencies and to increase glaze elasticity.

Tin oxide, the most commonly used tin compound, is nontoxic; but, in combination with toxic lead oxide, it has been widely used as "tin ash." In spite of its relatively high cost, tin oxide is used extensively by the artist-potter because of the warm character of the white produced in most glazes. In combination with other compounds, tin oxide is also used in some well-known ceramic stains such as tin-vanadium yellow; and in some pink, chrome stains.

Tin glazes with colorants added tend to be soft and subdued, when compared to similar glazes without tin.

Majolica and delftware are good examples that tin-opaqued glazes provide excellent bases for overglaze decoration. From eight to twelve per cent tin oxide assures that a transparent glaze will become opaque. From one to three per cent additions will generally cause translucency in the glaze.

White tin oxide will often dissolve in a glaze, provided that one per cent or less of the tin compound is added. Amounts of more than one per cent generally disperse as a finely divided, relatively insoluble, white pigment. Some formulas for tin glazes follow:

GLAZE I (Cone 015)
An opaque glaze with two to fifteen per cent additions of tin oxide.

Frit 14 (Hommel) 34.4
Frit 25 (Pemco) 56.6
Kaolin 9.0

GLAZE II (Cone 015)
A somewhat translucent glaze with two per cent tin oxide added; opaque with four to fifteen per cent additions.

Lithium Carbonate 9.4
Frit 14 (Hommel) 23.8
Frit 25 (Pemco) 38.2
Kaolin 9.6
Flint 19.0

GLAZE III (Cone 06)
A lightly translucent glaze with two to six per cent tin oxide added. Ten to fifteen per cent yields an opaque glaze.

Lithium Carbonate 14.1
Frit 14 (Hommel) 50.2
Kaolin 18.0
Flint 17.7

GLAZE IV (Cone 06)

An opaque glaze with two to four per cent tin oxide added. A somewhat stony matt glaze with ten to fifteen per cent tin oxide.

Gerstley Borate 22.8
Frit 25 (Pemco) 42.6
Kaolin 34.6

GLAZE V (Cone 06)

A greenish gray translucent glaze with two per cent tin oxide added, and opaque with six to fifteen per cent additions.

Lithium Carbonate 6.7
Frit 14 (Hommel) 15.1
Frit 25 (Pemco) 15.1
Albany Slip 63.1

GLAZE VI (Cone 4)

A somewhat translucent glaze with two to six per cent additions of tin oxide. Ten to fifteen per cent will yield an opaque glaze.

Wollastonite 23.3
Frit 14 (Hommel) 5.5
Frit 25 (Pemco) 46.4
Kaolin 8.4
Flint 16.4

GLAZE VII (Cone 4)

A somewhat translucent glaze with two per cent tin oxide added. With six to fifteen per cent it is opaque.

Whiting 23.6
Frit 25 (Pemco) 40.3
Kaolin 18.7
Flint 17.4

GLAZE VIII (Cone 4)

A satin matt glaze with two to fifteen per cent tin oxide added.

Lithium Carbonate 10.0
Whiting 5.0
Cryolite 6.0
Zinc Oxide 22.0
Kaolin 17.0
Titanium Dioxide 8.0
Flint 32.0

GLAZE IX (Cone 9)

A translucent glaze with additions of two to six per cent tin oxide; opaque with ten per cent; and matt with fifteen per cent.

Whiting 30.0
Frit 14 (Hommel) 15.0
Nepheline Syenite 55.0

Add: Bentonite 2.0

GLAZE X (Cone 9)

A somewhat translucent glaze with two per cent tin oxide added, but smoothly opaque with six to fifteen per cent.

Whiting 19.3
Spodumene 30.7
Kaolin 7.1
Flint 42.9

Using Kaolin in Simple Glazes

SIMPLY COMPOUNDED GLAZES of high stability may be made with kaolin as a major ingredient. Such glazes are inclined toward a broad range of firing temperatures, good hardness, and suitable viscosity during firing of the ware. They tend to have a matt appearance when the silica content is lowered and the alumina content is increased.

Calcined kaolin, rather than the raw clay, may be used to reduce the tendency to crack that a "high clay glaze" might have during drying. This could cause crawling of the glaze during firing. Calcining is achieved by firing kaolin to Cone 06 or higher. Calcining (pronounced cal-sign-ing) refers to the removal of chemically bonded water and other volatile gases by exposure to heat. A bisqued bowl is a good container for calcining ceramic materials in the kiln.

To provide for adequate suspension and adhesive qualities in the glaze prepared from calcined kaolin, two per cent bentonite may be added, as in the following glaze recipes:

GLAZE I (Cone 014)
A satin matt glaze

Gerstley Borate 73.6
Calcined Kaolin 26.4

Add: Bentonite 2.0

GLAZE II (Cone 06)
A clear glaze

Gerstley Borate 72.6
Calcined Kaolin 27.4

Add: Bentonite 2.0

GLAZE III (Cone 06)
A smooth cloudy glaze

Frit 14 (Hommel) 65.9
Calcined Kaolin 34.1

Add: Bentonite 2.0

GLAZE IV (Cone 06)
A clear glaze

Gerstley Borate 70.2
Calcined Kaolin 29.8

Add: Bentonite 2.0

GLAZE V (Cone 02)
A clear glaze

Frit 14 (Hommel) 63.2
Calcined Kaolin 36.8

Add: Bentonite 2.0

GLAZE VI (Cone 4)
A sugary glaze

Glass Cullet 65.2
Calcined Kaolin 34.8

Add: Bentonite 2.0

GLAZE VII (Cone 9)
A satin matt glaze

Wollastonite 50.2
Calcined Kaolin 49.8

Add: Bentonite 2.0

GLAZE VIII (Cone 9)
A satin matt glaze

Sodium Silicofluoride 46.1
Calcined Kaolin 53.9

Add: Bentonite 2.0

A Vapor Glazing Alternative

VAPOR GLAZING HAD ITS ORIGIN in Europe during the 12th century. Under the name of salt glazing, it was extensively used in the production of stoneware steins and other tableware. From there, its popularity spread throughout the Western world, largely as a result of the high stability of the glaze and its chemical or weather resistant qualities.

Today, the vapor glazing technique usually takes place in a downdraft, fuel-burning kiln constructed from hard firebrick or high alumina refractories. The technique is commonly used by potters to achieve the interesting textural character and integral appearance associated with salt glazes.

Moistened salt (sodium chloride) sometimes with borax added, is the substance originally employed in vapor glazing. The salt is added to the kiln atmosphere at the threshold of strong vitrification — at the maturing point of the clay body. The water used to moisten the salt, in addition to the water portion of burned fuel gases in the kiln, initiates a chemical reaction which produces vapors of sodium hydroxide (lye) and hydrochloric acid. At the high kiln temperatures, the sodium hydroxide vapors react chemically with the silica and alumina on the surface of ware to produce a very stable sodium-aluminum silicate glaze.

The hydrochloric acid vapor is one of the negative aspects of the process. Although non-poisonous, the vapor is corrosive and very irritating to the respiratory tract.

Vapor glazes may be produced at temperatures as low as Cone 05, but the most effective glazes are usually produced in the stoneware firing range. Bodies of high silica content are best suited to the process; other clays may be rendered acceptable with additions of flint.

As an ecologically attractive alternative to the hydrochloric acid vapor problem, the carbonate forms of the alkaline metals might be used instead of the chlorides. When carbonates are substituted, colorless, odorless, and non-poisonous carbon dioxide is released rather than the corrosive hydrochloric acid vapor.

A useful mixture of alkaline carbonates suitable for vapor glazing includes sodium carbonate (soda ash), potassium carbonate (pearl ash), and lithium carbonate. A sizable quantity of calcium carbonate (whiting) serves as a dispersing medium for the alkaline salts, although under some conditions, small amounts of this metal may migrate to the ware. Borax is also included, and a one per cent addition of bentonite aids adherence of the wet mix.

In preparation for a firing, the dry mix is converted to paste form with a small volume of water and sealed in packets of folded aluminum foil. This affords a convenient means of introducing the mixture into the fireboxes through a peephole or burner port. The size of the packets is dependent on the capacity of the kiln. A somewhat murky atmosphere should be maintained throughout the vapor glazing period. During the firing, the aluminum foil oxidizes to aluminum oxide, leaving a small amount of debris in the kiln.

Pyrometric cones can generally be utilized to determine the maturing point of ware preliminary to the addition of any glazing mixture; but, cones are rendered inaccurate during vapor glazing, and draw rings must be used to ascertain the course of glaze buildup.

Ceramic objects may be vapor glazed in a single firing on greenware, or bisque-fired pots may be used. A disadvantage of the process is that glaze cannot penetrate deep recesses. Suitable slip glazes are, therefore, usually applied to the interior of ware in conjunction with vapor glazing.

The color of the clay body subjected to vapor glazing can have a strong effect on the ultimate color of the glaze coating. A green hue may result when about three per cent green chromium oxide is used, and a blue with one or more per cent additions of cobalt oxide. Under reduction, however, large amounts of red iron oxide as a body colorant can result in splitting of the ware.

Colored or uncolored slips may be used effectively on both green and bisque-fired pots. Soluble salts such as iron chloride, cobalt nitrate, manganese sulfate, and copper sulfate may also be applied in about five per cent strength.

CLAY BODY (Cone 4-6, vapor glaze)
A white clay body containing considerable silica, for vapor glazing with carbonates.

Tennessee Ball Clay (O.M. #1) 65
Potash Feldspar 5
Talc 5
Frit 25 (Pemco) 5
Flint 20

CARBONATE VAPOR GLAZING MIXTURE
Borax 3
Lithium Carbonate 4
Soda Ash (Sodium Carbonate) 35
Pearl Ash (Potassium Carbonate) 7
Whiting 50
Bentonite 1

ALBANY GLAZE (Cone 4-6)
A recipe complementary to vapor glazing.

Nepheline Syenite 25
Albany Slip 75

Wide-Range-Firing Glazes

GLAZES WHICH PROVE FUNCTIONAL when fired throughout a wide range of cone levels can offer considerable flexibility. The use of wider-range glazes can often mitigate difficulties which grow out of temperature irregularities in the kiln, errors in judging the maturity of a glaze, intentional changes in firing procedures, and variations in the duration of firing. A number of technical factors are involved in determining the maturation of a glaze. The most important, undoubtedly, is glaze composition; other important factors are the fineness and uniformity of glaze particles, and the rate of firing.

In brief, wide-range-firing glazes generally contain a generous amount of alumina along with a multiple of metallic fluxes.

GLAZE I (Cone 018-010)
A clear glaze

Lithium Carbonate	10.0
Frit 259 (Hommel)	44.2
Frit 3134 (Ferro)	25.1
Kaolin	7.1
Flint	13.6

GLAZE II (Cone 02-5)
A matt glaze in the region of Cone 02, translucent at Cone 5.

Lithium Carbonate	2.9
Magnesium Carbonate	1.9
Strontium Carbonate	1.8
Whiting	13.2
Potash Feldspar	51.9
Kaolin	3.8
Flint	24.5

GLAZE III (Cone 08-1)
A translucent glaze

Gerstley Borate	50.0
Alumina Hydrate	4.0
Kaolin	12.0
Flint	34.0

GLAZE IV (Cone 04-4)
A matt glaze

Barium Carbonate	12.8
Lithium Carbonate	2.6
Strontium Carbonate	13.7
Zinc Oxide	7.7
Potash Feldspar	29.9
Kaolin	10.3
Flint	23.0

GLAZE V (Cone 06-4)
A matt glaze

Fluorspar	6.3
Gerstley Borate	8.4
Lithium Carbonate	4.2
Magnesium Carbonate	2.1
Wollastonite	21.1
Lepidolite	26.3
Kaolin	31.6

GLAZE VI (Cone 08-1)
A bright, chocolate, opaque glaze

Barium Carbonate	12.4
Lithium Carbonate	3.1
Strontium Carbonate	6.2
Wollastonite	10.9
Frit 14 (Hommel)	6.2
Barnard Clay	41.0
Flint	20.2

GLAZE VII (Cone 06-04)
A satin matt glaze

Lithium Carbonate	2.8
Zinc Oxide	3.8
Wollastonite	20.8
Cryolite	11.2
Kaolin	14.2
Flint	47.2

GLAZE VIII (Cone 012-04)
A clear glaze

Barium Carbonate	2.8
Whiting	12.7
Zinc Oxide	2.8
Frit 14 (Hommel)	9.8
Frit 25 (Pemco)	61.1
Nepheline Syenite	10.8

GLAZE IX (Cone 04-1)
A matt glaze

Magnesium Carbonate	6.3
Zinc Oxide	3.1
Wollastonite	17.3
Spodumene	29.2
Frit 14 (Hommel)	13.0
Kaolin	10.2
Flint	20.9

GLAZE X (Cone 016-08)
A clear glaze

Lithium Carbonate	5.0
Frit 25 (Pemco)	85.0
Whiting	5.0
Kaolin	5.0

GLAZE XI (Cone 06-4)
A satin matt glaze Cone 06-02, translucent Cone 1-4.

Barium Carbonate	9.2
Lithium Carbonate	1.7
Strontium Carbonate	6.9
Whiting	4.7
Zinc Oxide	3.8
Nepheline Syenite	10.5
Alumina Hydrate	11.0
Kaolin	12.1
Flint	40.1

GLAZE XII (Cone 08-02)
A satin matt glaze Cone 08-06, translucent Cone 04-02.

Barium Carbonate	14.3
Gerstley Borate	7.1
Whiting	3.6
Frit 25 (Pemco)	38.1
Kaolin	14.3
Flint	22.6

GLAZE XIII (Cone 08-4)
A translucent glaze

Barium Carbonate	4.3
Gerstley Borate	19.0
Lithium Carbonate	3.2
Strontium Carbonate	6.4
Whiting	4.4
Zinc Oxide	1.7
Frit 25 (Pemco)	17.5
Alumina Hydrate	3.4
Kaolin	11.2
Flint	28.9

GLAZE XIV (Cone 08-2)
A clear glaze

Barium Carbonate 4.8
Gerstley Borate 31.4
Lithium Carbonate 2.2
Strontium Carbonate 3.6
Zinc Oxide 3.9
Alumina Hydrate 3.8
Kaolin 12.5
Flint 37.8

GLAZE XV (Cone 08-5)
A satin matt glaze Cone 08-04, translucent Cone 04-5.

Gerstley Borate 18.2
Frit 25 (Pemco) 27.7
Alumina Hydrate 5.4
Kaolin 9.0
Flint 39.7

GLAZE XVI (Cone 1-9)
A glossy glaze

Barium Carbonate 4.0
Lithium Carbonate 2.0
Whiting 6.0
Zinc Oxide 8.0
Volcanic Ash 80.0

GLAZE XVII (Cone 1-9)
A satin matt glaze Cone 1-3, translucent Cone 4-9.

Wollastonite 22.8
Lepidolite 35.0
Kaolin 7.5
Flint 34.7

GLAZE XVIII (Cone 1-9)
A satin matt glaze at Cone 1, translucent Cone 2-9.

Magnesium Carbonate 2.6
Whiting 17.2
Potash Feldspar 48.3
Kaolin 4.3
Flint 27.6

GLAZE XIX (Cone 1-7)
A translucent glaze at Cone 1, becoming glossy at Cone 7.

Barium Carbonate 12.9
Magnesium Carbonate 1.5
Strontium Carbonate 5.0
Whiting 12.9
Zinc Oxide 1.5
Nepheline Syenite 29.5
Kaolin 4.0
Flint 32.7

Zinc Glazes

AS WITH MANY GLAZE MATERIALS used throughout history, zinc may be found in ancient glazes where it was introduced incidentally in unrefined materials, or purposely to obtain some of its advantages in the glaze. Its use as a flux and as a glaze modifier seems to have gained much impetus in the potting establishments of Bristol, England, and in the Rookwood Pottery in the United States.

Zinc glazes fired in the Cone 4-7 range are well adapted to the potter's needs. Such glazes contain major amounts of zinc and usually one or more of the alkaline metals — sodium, potassium, or lithium — as well as one or more of the alkaline earth metals — calcium, barium, strontium, or magnesium.

At the higher stoneware levels of firing, the volatility of zinc oxide makes the material less satisfactory as a major flux. As an auxiliary flux used to facilitate a smooth fusion transition from the sintered into the fully fused glaze, zinc has proved its value.

Zinc may serve as a flux in glazes firing as low as Cone 1, and it is sometimes used well below that point to contribute favorable qualities such as lower crazing, increased hardness, and resistance to abrasion.

When powerful fluxes like the alkaline metals or boron are used with zinc, glazes of considerably lower maturing points are produced. The zinc is also active in increasing glaze viscosity during the molten stage, and this tends to retard glaze fluidity during firing. (Glazes containing considerable zinc may obscure fine detail on ware.) The potter often utilizes zinc oxide as an opaquing and matting agent of superior quality, although clear glaze is obtainable from a well-fluxed batch.

Zinc glazes are often conditioned by the addition of considerable clay to render them useful on greenware. Both body and glaze may then be matured in a single firing.

When uncalcined zinc oxide is used in a glaze, faulting (particularly crawling) may result. The potter is well advised to calcine zinc oxide by heating it in a bisque-fired bowl during a low-temperature firing. The cooled material should then be sieved through a 100-mesh or finer screen before subsequent use.

Glazes containing a major portion of zinc may exhibit considerable color variations when combined with different oxides or stains. Some colors may be dulled, while others are often lightened or quite radically changed. Cobalt blues may be lightened in a zinc glaze; two per cent additions of nickel oxide may produce an icy blue color. Green chrome oxide in small amounts may impart a green hue to a zinc glaze, while larger additions may yield shades of brown. Opalescence in glazes with a high boron content may be promoted by the presence of zinc. Satin matts are often obtained if an excess of one third of the molecular metal units of a glaze is represented by zinc compounds.

The experimental potter may find in the following formulary, glazes to suit his ware:

GLAZE I (Cone 08)
A clear glaze

Lithium Carbonate 5.1
Zinc Oxide 18.6
Frit 25 (Pemco) 51.1
Kaolin 5.9
Flint 19.3

GLAZE II (Cone 08-01)
Matt at Cone 08, satin matt at Cone 01

Barium Carbonate 36.8
Lithium Carbonate 8.8
Zinc Oxide 13.3
Kaolin 14.5
Flint 26.6

GLAZE III (Cone 08-1)
A satin matt glaze at Cone 08, matt at Cone 04, and translucent at Cone 1.

Barium Carbonate 17.0
Lithium Carbonate 2.0
Whiting 10.5
Zinc Oxide 8.6
Nepheline Syenite 41.7
Flint 20.2

Add: Bentonite 1.0

GLAZE IV (Cone 1-9)
A matt glaze at Cone 1, translucent Cone 4-6, bright and clear at Cone 9.

Whiting 8.0
Zinc Oxide 6.5
Potash Feldspar 59.6
Kaolin 13.8
Flint 12.1

GLAZE V (Cone 1-9)
An opaque matt glaze at Cone 1, translucent Cone 6-9.

Whiting 7.3
Zinc Oxide 8.4
Potash Feldspar 57.3
Kaolin 15.2
Flint 11.8

GLAZE VI (Cone 01-9)
A bright matt glaze at Cone 01, translucent Cone 4-6, and transparent at Cone 9.

Whiting 9.0
Zinc Oxide 9.7
Potash Feldspar 50.1
Kaolin 17.8
Flint 13.4

GLAZE VII (Cone 1-4)
A marked matt glaze at Cone 1, satin matt at Cone 4.

Lithium Carbonate 10.0
Whiting 4.6
Zinc Oxide 22.0
Kaolin 17.7
Titanium Dioxide 7.4
Flint 38.3

GLAZE VIII (Cone 4-9)
A satin matt glaze

Barium Carbonate 22.1
Whiting 7.6
Zinc Oxide 6.5
Potash Feldspar 50.4
Kaolin 4.7
Flint 8.7

GLAZE IX (Cone 1-4)
A satin matt glaze

Whiting 10.6
Zinc Oxide 10.2
Wollastonite 13.9
Potash Feldspar 47.2
Kaolin 18.1

GLAZE X (Cone 4-9)
A matt glaze at Cone 4, translucent at Cone 9

Strontium Carbonate 16.6
Zinc Oxide 9.7
Potash Feldspar 34.3
Kaolin 11.8
Flint 27.6

GLAZE XI (Cone 6-9)
A translucent glaze at Cone 6, transparent at Cone 9.

Whiting 8.9
Zinc Oxide 8.4
Volcanic Ash 82.7

Add: Bentonite 1.0

GLAZE XII (Cone 4-9)
A matt glaze Cone 4-6, translucent at Cone 9

Whiting 6.8
Zinc Oxide 7.7
Potash Feldspar 60.5
Kaolin 14.0
Flint 11.0

Temperature Equivalents

for Orton Pyrometric Cones as determined at the National Bureau of Standards

Cone Number	Large Cones Temperature Rise Per Hour		Small Cones Temperature Rise Per Hour	
	60°C	108°F	300°C	540°F
022	585°C	1085°F	630°C	1165°F
021	602	1116	643	1189
020	625	1157	666	1231
019	668	1234	723	1333
018	696	1285	752	1386
017	727	1341	784	1443
016	764	1407	825	1517
015	790	1454	843	1549
014	834	1533	870	1596
013	869	1596	880	1615
012	866	1591	900	1650
011	886	1627	915	1680
010	887	1629	919	1686
09	915	1679	955	1751
08	945	1733	983	1801
07	973	1783	1008	1846
06	991	1816	1023	1873
05	1031	1888	1062	1944
04	1050	1922	1098	2008
03	1086	1987	1131	2068
02	1101	2014	1148	2098
01	1117	2043	1178	2152
1	1136	2077	1179	2154
2	1142	2088	1179	2154
3	1152	2106	1196	2185
4	1168	2134	1209	2208
5	1177	2151	1221	2230
6	1201	2194	1255	2291
7	1215	2219	1264	2307
8	1236	2257	1300	2372
9	1260	2300	1317	2403
10	1285	2345	1330	2426
11	1294	2361	1336	2437
12	1306	2383	1355	2471

From the Edward Orton, Jr., Ceramic Foundation, Columbus, Ohio